# CRICUT FOR BEGINNERS

A Step by Step Guide to Master Your Cricut Machine, Design Space and Original Cricut Project Ideas for Beginners

*Fairy Creations*

© **Copyright 2020 by Fairy Creations**
**All rights reserved.**

This document is geared towards providing exact and reliable information with regards to the topic and issue covered. The publication is sold with the idea that the publisher is not required to render accounting, officially permitted, or otherwise, qualified services. If advice is necessary, legal or professional, a practiced individual in the profession should be ordered.

- From a Declaration of Principles which was accepted and approved equally by a Committee of the American Bar Association and a Committee of Publishers and Associations.

In no way is it legal to reproduce, duplicate, or transmit any part of this document in either electronic means or in printed format. Recording of this publication is strictly prohibited and any storage of this document is not allowed unless with written permission from the publisher. All rights reserved.

The information provided herein is stated to be truthful and consistent, in that any liability, in terms of inattention or otherwise, by any usage or abuse of any policies, processes, or directions contained within is the solitary and utter responsibility of the recipient reader. Under no circumstances will any legal responsibility or blame be held against the publisher for any reparation, damages, or monetary loss due to the information herein, either directly or indirectly.

Respective authors own all copyrights not held by the publisher.

The information herein is offered for informational purposes solely, and is universal as so. The presentation of the information is without contract or any type of guarantee assurance.

The trademarks that are used are without any consent, and the publication of the trademark is without permission or backing by the trademark owner. All trademarks and brands within this book are for clarifying purposes only and are the owned by the owners themselves, not affiliated with this document

# Table of Contents

Introduction .......................................................................... 5

Chapter 1: What is a Cricut machine? [The basics of Cricut (what is a Cricut?)Types, difference, uniqueness] ................. 6

Chapter 2: Best materials that can be worked on using a Cricut machine ................................................................................ 21

Chapter 3: Simple operations that you can do the Cricut cutter machine .............................................................................. 37

Chapter 4: How to master the use of integrated "Design Space" ............................................................................... 70

Chapter 5: How to work with vinyl .................................... 120

Chapter 6: Simple projects with vinyl and card stock ....... 132

Chapter 7: Instruction to upload images with a Cricut machine ................................................................................. 140

Chapter 8: How to make stickers ...................................... 150

Chapter 9: Cricut scrapbooking ......................................... 178

Chapter 10: How to choose a new Cricut machine (powerful tips for how to buy a Cricut machine) ............................... 185

Chapter 11: How to use a Cricut cutter and choose the right cartridge to purchase (depending on needs and budget) .. 204

Chapter 12: How to make modifications to your design by editing the images and fonts ............................................ 218

Conclusion ........................................................................ 242

# Introduction

Hey there,

If you are a fan of crafts and DIY, this book is for you. In this book, I have broken down the numerous frequently asked question about how to operate a Cricut machine. The Cricut machine is a cutting edge device that enables you to make fancy and useful art and crafts. You can personally customize your wares at the comfort of your own home with this device, and this book will teach you how.

If peradventure you haven't purchased a Cricut machine, this book holds a guide on how to go about getting one that will suit your need and purpose. It will also teach you how to set it up; what goes where, and how to go about crafting.

It is a compendium of knowledge about the Cricut machine, in the most conversational terms possible. You can read it from start to finish. Or you could scroll through the easy to understand chapters to read up what you need. Whatever you do, don't forget to unleash your craftsmanship with the helpful tips I've written here.

# Chapter 1:
# What is a Cricut machine? [The basics of Cricut (what is a Cricut?)Types, difference, uniqueness]

Perhaps you got a Cricut machine for Christmas, or a birthday, however, it's despite everything sitting in its case. Or on the other hand, perhaps you're an eager crafter searching for a straightforward apparatus to make creating simpler. Or then again maybe you've seen massive amounts of fresh task pictures on Pinterest and pondered "How the hell do they cut those multifaceted structures? I wanna do that!" Or perhaps you've known about Cricut. However, you're asking "What is a Cricut machine, and what would you be able to do with it?" Well, you're in the ideal spot; today I will acquaint you with the Cricut Explore Air machine and enlighten you regarding all the cool things it can do!

What is a Cricut machine, and what would you be able to do with it?

I initially utilized a Cricut path back in school. I was an RA, and our occupant staff office had a Cricut machine and a couple of cartridges that we used for removing letters and shapes to make fun signs and gathering improvements. I believed that thing was SO COOL. Yet, Cricut machines have grown up a great deal since I've been in school, and they are much cooler at this point!

There are no more cartridges; all thing is done carefully with the goal that you can utilize any text style or shape that is on your PC. Also, the majority of the Cricut machines work over wifi or Bluetooth, so you can structure from your iPhone or iPad, just as from your PC! The Cricut machines are anything but difficult to utilize, absolutely flexible, and only constrained by your own imagination!

What Is A Cricut Machine?

The Cricut Explore Air is a bite the dust cutting machine (otherwise known as speciality plotter or cutting machine). You can consider it like a printer; you make a picture or plan on your PC and afterwards send it to the machine. Then again, actually, as opposed to printing your project, the Cricut machine removes it of whatever material you need! The Cricut Explore Air cut paper, vinyl, texture, make froth, sticker paper, false cowhide, and the sky is the limit from there!

What is a Cricut machine, and what would you be able to do with it?

Indeed, on the off chance that you need to utilize a Cricut like a printer, it can do that as well! There is an extra opening in the machine, and you can stack a marker in there and afterwards have the Cricut "draw" your structure for you. It's ideal for getting an exquisite transcribed look if your penmanship isn't too extraordinary.

What is a Cricut machine, and what would you be able to do with it?

The Explore arrangement of Cricut machines permits you to get to a large computerized library of "cartridges" rather than utilizing physical cartridges, as I did in school. This implies you can use Cricut Design Space (their online structure programming) to take any content or shape from the library and send it to your Cricut to be removed. You can even transfer your own structures in the event that you need!

The Cricut Explore Air can slice materials up to 12" wide and has a little cutting sharp edge mounted inside the machine. At the point when you're prepared to remove something, you load the material onto a clingy tangle and burden the knot into the computer. The tangle holds the equipment set up while the Cricut cutting edge disregards the material and cuts it. At the point when it completes, you empty the knot from the machine, strip your undertaking off the clingy tangle, and you're all set!

What is a Cricut machine, and what would you be able to do with it?

With a Cricut machine, the conceivable outcomes are inestimable! All you need is a Cricut machine, something to cut, Design Space, and your own inventiveness!

CURRENT CRICUT CUTTING MACHINES

There are five Cricut cutting machines. (The base costs for the devices are in the blueprint beneath, yet click these connections to Amazon—you can regularly spare yourself a considerable amount!)

Cricut Joy (propelling 3/1/2020)

Cricut Maker

Cricut Explore One

Cricut Explore Air

Cricut Explore Air 2

Inheritance machines that aren't being sold any longer incorporate Cricut Gypsy, Cricut Cake, Cricut Personal, Cricut Expression, Cricut Expression 2, and the first Cricut Explore.

Note that there is additionally Cricut Cuttlebug, which is another kind of machine out and out, and is principally beyond words and decorating. It was ended as of spring 2019.

CRICUT MACHINE COMPARISON CHART

Before we broadly expound on each machine, open a PDF of this useful correlation diagram by tapping on it! At that point, see beneath for inside and out conversations of each device.

Cricut Comparison Chart - Hey, Let's Make Stuff

CRICUT JOY

Cricut Joy

On February 12, 2020, Cricut declared their most up to date cutting machine, Cricut Joy. I was fortunate enough to travel out to Salt Lake City to find out about the machine before it was reported. I wasn't sure from the start in the event that I would utilize a little machine. However, it immediately prevailed upon me.

Cricut Joy is a conservative small cutting machine, not exactly a large portion of the size of Cricut Explore and Cricut Maker. It's pared-down a piece from the other Cricut machines, with a solitary cutting edge and pen holder. The cut width is 4.5".

Yet, don't let its size numb-skull you—it has a fabulous time new highlights! Two major ones are sans tangle cutting, which implies you can slice up to 20' (truly, twenty feet) of "Brilliant vinyl" in a single go. Cricut Joy likewise has a Card Mat, making it overly easy to make cards for a wide range of events.

The value purpose of $179 may even now be somewhat high for some crafters, especially since a portion of the capacities are slightly restricted. Be that as it may, Cricut Joy is ideal for practically the entirety of your fundamental Cricut makes, remembering iron for vinyl, cement vinyl, writable names, and cardstock.

Best for: producers without a devoted art space, new Cricut clients threatened by the bigger Cricut machines, or as a buddy machine to your Explore or Maker.

CRICUT MAKER

Cricut producer

Cricut Maker is Cricut's best in a glass cutting machine. It appears to be like the Explore line of machines, yet it has been re-structured from the base up. It does everything Cricut Explore will do, yet with included highlights.

Cricut Maker cuts unbonded texture (so you needn't bother with a stabilizer as you do with the Cricut Explore line) utilizing the little Rotary Blade. It cuts thicker materials (up to 3/32") like balsa wood and thick cowhide utilizing the Knife Blade. It can score a wide range of materials utilizing the Scoring Wheel (a stage up from the Scoring Stylus).

In July 2019, four new instruments were declared. You can perceive how to utilize every one of these instruments in these posts:

The Engraving Tool

The Debossing Tool

The Wavy Rotary Tool

The Perforation Tool

Cricut Maker's versatile device framework is worked in light of extension—which means it was worked to utilize apparatuses that Cricut hasn't concocted at this point! They have twelve extra devices in testing—so this machine will accomplish increasingly more as new instruments are discharged.

The value point is the most elevated in the Cricut line—$399, some of the time marked down for $349. In any case, in case you're a genuine crafter who likes to utilize an assortment of materials, or on the off chance that you are a sewing devotee, an ardent paper crafter, or maybe even a carpenter, this machine is for you.

I reviewed a long post about Cricut Maker—I went to the enormous discharge occasion and chatted with numerous individuals on the Cricut group about it.

BEST FOR Crafters who need everything—particularly the individuals who cut texture or cut thicker materials.

CRICUT EXPLORE AIR 2

Cricut Explore Air 2

This is the Cricut Explore that I have (notwithstanding my Maker), and I should state that I love it. At $299, however, I realize it may be out of the value scope of certain clients.

There are two contrasts between the Cricut Explore Air 2 and the Cricut Explore Air. One is large, and one is little. The large one is that the Air 2 will slice and review to multiple times quicker than the Air. It's not all materials. However, it functions admirably for most materials that you'd need to cut. This is a distinct advantage on the off chance that you utilize your Cricut a great deal—you recognize what it resembles to sit tight for a since a long time ago eliminate or compose position to wrap up!

The little contrast is that the Air 2 arrives in a gigantic assortment of hues to coordinate your speciality space. For a few, it's absolutely not worth spending the extra $50. However, it may be in the event that you simply LOVE one of the numerous hues available today.

BEST FOR: Users who claim a creating business will truly see the speed distinction, and it will have any kind of effect with how rapidly they can deliver things for customers.

CRICUT EXPLORE AIR

Cricut Explore Air

Cricut Explore Air is a stage down, but offers you the two things that the Cricut Explore One beneath doesn't—it is Bluetooth-empowered, so you don't need to plug it into your gadget, and it has the optional instrument holder, so you can compose and cut or score and cut simultaneously. At $249, I believe it merits the move up to get these two additional highlights, yet you may conclude that they aren't justified, despite any potential benefits for what you need to do with your Cricut.

BEST FOR: Most clients will see this as a proficient machine for all that they have to do.

CRICUT EXPLORE ONE

Cricut Explore One

Cricut Explore One is the most essential and prudent machine that Cricut offers, and at $199 the cost can't be beaten. It has the entirety of the exact cutting, composing, and scoring capacities of the Explore Air machines, and you can cut no different materials (there are more than 100!). None of the three machines requires cartridges. However, you can utilize your heritage cartridges in every one of them.

Be that as it may, it has two remarkable contrasts.

The first is that it isn't Bluetooth-empowered, which implies that you have to run a line from your gadget to your Cricut to interface the two. Not a serious deal, however, it very well may be somewhat of a torment contingent upon how your making space is set up. My unique Cricut Explore (which is never again accessible) wasn't remote, and it wasn't the apocalypse (that being stated, I presently truly love having my Cricut on one side of the room and me on the other at my work area!).

The second is that there is anything but a twofold apparatus cartridge, so you can't compose and cut (or score and cut) in a similar pass. You can at present compose and score, you simply need to do it independently. Once more, not a tremendous torment except if you're composing and cutting or scoring and cutting a great deal. In case you're simply cutting, this won't have that a lot of an effect.

BEST FOR: Users who chiefly need to cut utilizing their Cricuts, and the individuals who have a making space where their gadget is set up close to their Cricut machine.

I trust you discovered this little breakdown accommodating.

What Can I Make With A Cricut Machine?

Literally, there are LOTS of things you can do with a Cricut machine! It is highly unlikely I could get even rundown all the conceivable outcomes, yet here are a couple of mainstream sorts of undertakings to give you a thought of what the machine can do.

Cut out enjoyment shapes and letters for scrapbooking.

Make custom, high-quality cards for any exceptional event (here's a model)

Plan a onesie or a shirt (here's a model)

Make a calfskin arm ornament.

Make buntings and other gathering beautifications.

Make your own stencils for painting (here's a model)

Make a vinyl sticker for your vehicle window.

Mark stuff in your storeroom, or in a den

Make monogram pads

Make your own Christmas adornments (here's a model)

Address an envelope

Enhance a mug, cup, or tumbler (here's a model)

Engraving glass at home (here's a model)

Make your own divider decals.

Make a painted wooden sign.

Make your own window sticks.

Cut appliqués or blanket squares

Make decals for a stand blender.

… and huge amounts of different ventures that are too various to even think about listing!

Here are the Cricut machines I talked about right now; the pictures beneath to discover increasingly about each machine. Also, in case you're hoping to purchase an amazing creating device, I enthusiastically prescribe the Cricut Explore machines! I utilize mine essentially consistently, and it rocks!

# Chapter 2: Best materials that can be worked on using a Cricut machine

Best materials for Cricut machines

It's pretty generally realizing that Cricut machines can cut materials like vinyl and paper. However, do you know that these little powerhouses can lower so significantly more than that?! I'm talking everything from wood to kinds of plastic and textures!

Not yet acquainted with Cricut? Make sure to peruse my Beginners Guide to Cricut Terms here!

Or then again perhaps you know about what the machine can cut, yet battle to discover these Cricut materials in create stores and wish you realized where to look on the web.

Indeed, today is your day of reckoning because beneath I am covering a rundown of explicit Cricut materials, where to discover them and what edge they work best with!

A portion of these Cricut materials can be utilized with more than one sharp edge. Cricut cutting edges are so adaptable! If you are generally new to Cricut, you may very well be shocked at what it can cut!

I will reveal to you that with regards to sifting through where to purchase the wide assortment of Cricut materials, that can be utilized for your undertakings, you are ideal for keeping away from first steam make stores, particularly if you need to set aside cash. Most speciality stores value things, similar to vinyl and calfskin 2x higher for a large portion of the sum.

I additionally have made a cutting aide for Cricut clients. Download my free cutting diagram in my crafter's asset library! Forefront Crafter individuals as of now get access to this in their rewards!

The best tenderfoot's guide for Cricut

So how about we plunge into all the Cricut materials!

What does Cricut cut? Which sharp edges do you use for texture, vinyl or wood?

Cricut Materials that can be utilized with the Fine-point sharp edge

The materials recorded in the segment underneath all function admirably with the fine-point Cricut sharp edge. Effectively modify the pre-named settings on the dial or in Design Space to coordinate what you are utilizing. I will likewise take note of the settings underneath.

Iron-on vinyl

Iron-on vinyl is dominatingly utilized on things that are texture situated somehow or another, for example, shirts, totes, fabric napkins, and so on. Look at a board brimming with thoughts here!

For iron-on vinyl, make sure to utilize the iron-on setting on your Cricut.

Iron-on vinyl (a.k.a heat move vinyl or HTV) is an outright most loved for most Cricut clients and functions admirably with a fine-point cutting edge, yet what is a portion of the absolute best iron-on vinyl to utilize?

1. Siser Heat Transfer Vinyl – Easy to weed and they have been around for quite a while! Siser additionally has sparkle vinyl alternatives, designed vinyl, flower designs just as holographic choices! Shop them all here!

2. Cricut Heat Transfer Vinyl – Cricut's vinyl are incredible because they are made for Cricut and my Cricut. They additionally offer a wide assortment of hues and surfaces like sparkle.

3. My Vinyl Direct – Vinyl Direct has something beyond HTV significantly, so I will point you back to it more than once. They have a lot of examples, hues, and surfaces to shop!

4. Firefly Heat Transfer Vinyl – Firefly is broadly known and confided in the brand. In addition to the fact that it has extraordinary surveys, they have a fabulous choice! What's more, on the off chance that you are searching for exceptional fluffy ran vinyl or sparkle vinyl they have you secured!

5. Distinction Heat Transfer Vinyl – This brand is extraordinary when you are chasing for a wide choice of hues. The other advantage of this brand is that it is less expensive than a few different options on the off chance that you are on a tight spending plan!

Tangle to utilize: Generally, the standard hold tangle will work with all types of vinyl.

Cement Vinyl – Use Vinyl Setting

Cement vinyl is a nearby most loved to the HTV. There are many utilizations for glue vinyl, for example, divider decals, mugs, decorations, compartments, divider craftsmanship, and so on. Here are the absolute best brands beneath for AV!

There are fundamentally 2 classes of glue vinyl – perpetual outside and removable indoor – with different sorts inside every classification. Vinyl will consistently be explained as one of those sorts, and you should utilize appropriately to the undertaking for best outcomes.

For instance, removable glue vinyl would work incredibly as a removable divider decal. In contrast, changeless vinyl will work better for a wood sign you intend to hold tight your front entryway.

For glue vinyl, you will, by and large, utilize the vinyl setting on your Cricut.

1. Oracal Vinyl – This vinyl is my own top decision when I am pondering beginning a cement vinyl venture. The prophet is viewed as the business head with regards to make vinyl. This vinyl is intended to a years ago. You can likewise discover moves of this on Vinyl Direct here in both reflexive or matte!

2. Cricut Adhesive Vinyl – Cricut is as yet an extraordinary go-to asset for AV. In general, Cricut tends to be increasingly expensive. Still, there are times that I locate a superior shade in shading I am looking for with Cricut's vinyl.

3. Articulations Vinyl – Expressions vinyl is another most loved and simple to utilize. They have a decent shading choice of sparkle also!

Sparkle 12 "x24" Vinyl Sheets

4. Glad Crafters – Honestly this is only an upbeat spot site – you will discover vinyl of various kinds and a lot other art-related supplies!

Tangle to utilize: Standard hold fills in also for cement vinyl.

Cardstock

Paper and cardstock are precious to me since I love to make paper blossoms. Truth be told, you can gain admittance to my entire library of treats when you join! Snap the pink catch underneath.

Snap HERE TO GAIN ACCESS

Be that as it may, my point is that I know cardstock well. So my preferred assets are beneath.

While creating with cardstock, set the dial to cardstock or one setting further to one side on the dial for anything over 65-pound cardstock.

1. Memories cardstock – Recollection is a brand by Michael's speciality store, yet they can likewise be discovered on the web! I utilize this brand the most for my papercrafts.

2. Savage Universal paper rolls – I as of late found how great Savage paper functions for paper creating. Although it appears to be somewhat expensive forthright, it keeps going so any longer!

3. Paper and that's just the beginning – Paper and more is a believed asset I have utilized, and I love the more one of a kind hues they have.

4. Cards and Pockets – This site has been with me for a considerable length of time. In light of current circumstances, the shading choices are unusual to most.

Tangle to use for cardstock paper: Standard grasp

Extra Fine-Point Blade Materials

We should likewise cover different materials that work with the fine-point edge and furthermore the standard hold tangle:

Meagre chipboard – useful for wreaths or large letter or number patterns. Set dial to custom and select chipboard.

Slight banner board – use for ventures with foundations or enormous patterns. The dial ought to be set to the banner board.

Stencil Sheets – Create your own client stencils with your Cricut! I, for the most part, have utilized the cardstock setting for stencil material however on the off chance that you purchase an alternate brand that is thicker, at that point 6 mil you may go up on the weight.

Sticker paper or tattoo paper – If you are utilizing the print and cut element, consider doing it on sticker or tattoo paper for an enjoyable venture. I like to cut my own organizer stickers! Utilize the cardstock setting for these too with the fine-point cutting edge.

Vellum – Vellum is simply one more sort of paper that usually is fragile and translucent. It works extraordinary for any assortment of papercrafts. For vellum, make a point to set the dial to paper or vinyl.

Cellophane – Every sometimes I discover a venture I am making needs an adaptable and clear like material – cellophane works extraordinary for that, and your Cricut can cut it! Cellophane should be cut at the lightest setting, typically paper or the one speck before it.

Rundown of materials that Cricut Explore and Maker can cut!

Profound cut cutting edge – What Can I cut?

For every one of the materials underneath, you will need to set you dial or machine to custom and search the name of the material to set the correct cut weight.

Chipboard – If you need thicker chipboard, then what the fine-point cutting edge can deal with, at that point set your profound slice edge to work!

Elastic – Want to make your own stamps? You thoroughly can with this incredible elastic and the deep cut sharp edge.

Wood facade embellishments – You may have the option to utilize a fine-point sharp edge with the wood facade on the off chance that it is sufficiently flimsy, yet likely will need the profound cutting edge by and large.

Magnets – Creating your own magnets can be extremely fun. A remarkable educator thankfulness blessing truth be told.

Cowhide – Leather is extremely popular at this moment, particularly those great calfskin studs!

Art froth – Foam is particularly magnificent for kids creates. Pre-cut a lot of fun shapes and have your children appreciate some sly enjoyment time! I love this undertaking here!

Matboard – Matboard is basic cardboard, however, more pleasant. So any undertaking you need to utilize cardboard for can work with the profound cut cutting edge!

Felt sheets – Love felt blossoms or artworks? At that point, let your Cricut accomplish the work for you! You can likewise do felt sheets!

Sparkle cardstock – I love my sparkle cardstock for a wide range of tasks. I have cut it with the fine-point sharp edge; however, the profound works better particularly with the stout sparkle paper. Speciality stores frequently have a few or utilize the connection I gave!

Settings: For the materials right now will presumably choose custom for vast numbers of them and afterwards determine in Design Space which one you are utilizing on the cut screen. Configuration Space has a setting for the majority of these alternatives at any rate.

Mats: For things like felt and cowhide, the textured tangle will be ideal. On the off chance that you are cutting chipboard, sparkle cardstock, wood facade or tangle board a standard tangle will by and large work fine. Elastic or magnets may require the solid hold tangle.

Texture Blade – What Can I Cut?

The sharp texture edge is truly explicit to texture, and you will, for the most part, keep the feel setting set-up on the dial. Here are a couple of my preferred texture spots to shop. You can likewise cut texture with the 2 past cutting edges talked about however I suggest checking out the surface proposed sharp edge!

Spoonflower – If you need A LOT of texture to pick from or to specially craft your own texture in a couple of short snaps then Spoonflower is the best approach

Joann Fabrics – Many of you have presumably known about Joann's Fabrics. They have been around quite a while, and some of you may have a store close by. On the off chance that you don't, you can shop here on the web!

Texture Direct – If you need a significant site loaded with taste and at discount costs, at that point, make certain to look at texture direct. I have bought velvet from them for some fall pumpkin creates and adored it!

Tangle to utilize: Fabric holds tangle or standard grasp.

Blade (Cricut Maker just) – What Can I Cut?

With the blade cutting edge (Cricut Maker no one but) you can cut a lot of comparable Cricut materials likewise with the profound sharp edge, BUT the thing that matters is that it can cut 2-3x thicker materials then the Explore can deal with! Actually, the blade cutting edge can slice material up to 3mm thick! All the more significantly, it does it with a progressively exact and clean accuracy cut then the profound cut sharp edge with Explore.

Thick balsa wood or basswood – this material is phenomenal for removing wood edges, decorations, or in any event, constructing little articles like a perch room!

Full calfskin – The blade cutting edge has been commended for how well and clean it cuts thicker cowhide materials. So on the off chance that you need to make those great cowhide studs or perhaps a grasp handbag then this is energizing! Coincidentally, look at this gold and silver calfskin!

Thick chipboard – If you need a thicker chipboard material, the blade cutting edge can take a jar of that.

Thick art froth – Up your thickness with the blade sharp edge with utilizing heavier speciality froths!

Tangle to utilize: A crisp standard grasp tangle will work for materials more slender than 1 mm yet, for the most part, the blade sharp edge is used on thicker materials, so I prescribe the solid hold tangle. In case you're utilizing something like 3 mm balsa wood you may likewise need to use some painter's tape around the edges to guarantee it doesn't slide mid-cut.

Settings: For the wood, chipboard, and cowhide there are settings you can choose with you click on "see all materials" in Design Space. Art foam, as a rule, functions admirably on the thicker cardstock setting.

Turning Blade (Cricut Maker just) – What Can I cut?

Washi Sheets – Washi Sheets are magnificent claim to fame papers. As a rule, they have some excellent times surfaces or prints on them. They work perfectly for cards!

Crepe paper – Can you say pure crepe paper blossoms?!

Report this advertisement

Stopper – Cork can be sensitive to cut, so the sharp turning edge is perfect!

Tissue paper – Cut tissue paper with as well! Make a point to pick a more exceptional document like the one connected here.

Tender textures – Fabrics that are increasingly fragile like tulle, organza, and trim are a solid match for the sharp rotating edge.

Tangle to utilize: You can use a texture grasp tangle for light textures and stopper, yet use a standard or light hold tangle for crepe and light for tissue paper.

Settings: Delicate textures ought to be set to the texture choice setting, while the tissue, crepe, and washi paper ought to be set on their named setting inside custom settings.

Amazing! That was a long article, folks! I trust this provides you with some reliable guidance for discovering Cricut materials, which sharp edge to utilize, tangle and settings!

# Chapter 3: Simple operations that you can do the Cricut cutter machine

I love finding out about new Cricut tasks and Cricut Explore Air 2 Projects. Yet, some Cricut makes appear to be further developed than others. I set up this rundown with Easy Cricut Projects for Beginners to help other people discover Cricut instructional exercises for apprentices and free Cricut ventures. A large portion of the projects highlighted right now be caused utilizing a Cricut To investigate Air and Cricut Explore Air 2, yet a proportion of these apprentice ventures require a Cricut Maker Machine (Cricut tenderfoot activities using texture).

Continue perusing to discover Cricut Explore Air ventures, Cricut Air 2 activities, Cricut vinyl ventures, farmhouse Cricut ventures for amateurs, and that's only the tip of the iceberg!

Figuring out how to utilize your Cricut is extremely simple and fun once you get its hang. I love using Cricut Design Space print at that point cut highlights. If you don't have a Cricut Access Membership, I energetically prescribe it. I've had a Cricut Access Membership for a considerable length of time, and it's unquestionably worth the expense for all the advantages!

If you don't have the Cricut Access Membership, I emphatically prescribe it since you'll gain admittance to a great many pictures, several textual styles, 10% off your acquisition of materials, machines, apparatuses, and so forth... in addition to 10% off premium pictures, text styles, instant activities, AND you get need in the part care line!

This is the Cricut Machine that I claim and use it for natural materials. I likewise have this machine, yet I just use it to cut texture.

My preferred online asset to discover SVG records to make Cricut make ventures is DesignBundles.net!

Cricut Basics

Simple Cricut Projects for Beginners

These Cricut venture thoughts will present all the Cricut make thoughts that you can make as an amateur Cricut novice. Practically the entirety of the beneath Cricut machine ventures incorporate Cricut instructional exercises for fledgelings. How about we begin...

Cricut Paper Crafts

Paper makes are one of the first ventures I made utilizing my Cricut machine. Snatch some card stock, (either 60 lb or 110 lb) from your nearby speciality store (my preferred art supply stores are Michael's Stores, Hobby Lobby, Cutcardstock.com, Amazon, and Cricut.com) and begin making stuff!

Cricut Paper Flowers

Take a stab at making these paper blossom corsages! There is somewhat of an expectation to absorb information with regards to making paper blossoms; however, once you get its hang, you will never purchase another silk/counterfeit bloom again!

My companion Abbi from Abbi Kirstin Collections makes the most excellent monster blossoms, and she shares free layouts and instructional exercises on the most proficient method to reproduce them. She likewise has a book on the speciality of making Giant blossoms that I energetically suggest you look at!

Cricut Paper Greeting Cards

I purchased my first Cricut machine to make welcoming cards (and those welcome cards gave pay through my Etsy shop!). The principal undertaking you make utilizing Cricut ought to be a welcome card (Cricut even sends you materials and directions to make your first welcome card venture!). There are such a large number of welcome cards accessible in Cricut Design Space Make-It-Now posts!

On the off chance that you don't have the Cricut Access Membership, I enthusiastically prescribe it since you'll gain admittance to a considerable number of pictures, many text styles, 10% off your acquisition of materials, machines, devices, and so on… in addition to 10% off premium pictures, textual styles, instant undertakings, AND you get need in the part care line!

I love glancing through the Make-it-now extends on Cricut, and the welcome cards are too simple when you need a very late Birthday card like this cake card I made as of late!

Cricut ventures, Cricut Explore Air 2 Projects, Cricut Explore Air Projects, Cricut Explore Projects, free Cricut ventures, Cricut vinyl ventures, Cricut venture thoughts,

Cricut Air 2 tasks, Cricut machine ventures, Cricut Explore ventures for apprentices, Cricut instructional exercises for novices, Cricut for tenderfoots, Cricut ventures fledgeling, Cricut ventures learner texture, farmhouse Cricut ventures amateur, Cricut mugs novice, DIY Cricut ventures novice, vinyl Cricut Projects

Cricut Cardstock Home Decor

It's so natural to cut paper shapes and use them in your home stylistic layout. Look at how I utilized my Cricut machine to cut these paper bats and used tape to tie down them to this Dollar Store Burlap Wreath...

This Halloween wreath was extremely simple and modest to make! I got the provisions at the Dollar store and hand slice the leaves in hues to coordinate our home stylistic layout. It turned out so charming!

I additionally utilized the equivalent Cricut cut paper bats on our front entryway (I used 110 lb. substantial cardstock). We have a secured patio, and the paper bats were in such acceptable condition in the wake of showing on our front entryway that I got them together to utilize again one year from now.

Keep your Halloween front entryway adornments essential this year while making creepy Halloween designs for your Fall front entryway. These are innovative thoughts for custom made Halloween style that is likewise modest Halloween stylistic theme and goes with a greenish-blue front entryway. The outcome is Simple Halloween Front Porch Decor that includes the ideal bit of Halloween open-air designs.

What's more, I utilized the equivalent Cricut slice bats on this divider to brighten our home for Halloween. I got such a large number of praises (even an offer from Cricut!) on Instagram during Fall 2018 when I told the best way to utilize these paper bats in Halloween stylistic theme.

This Halloween Banner and Halloween home stylistic layout are so natural to make, and you can discover supplies at the dollar store. I love her free printables, including this bison plaid standard!

During Valentine's Day, I cut some paper hearts and utilized them to course down a divider... Oh, and those pink cushions (The XOXO and heart) were made with my Cricut Maker machine! I attempt to utilize Cricut to make my own home stylistic layout things before burning through cash on a home stylistic theme. The vast majority of the stylish stylistic layout you can purchase is typically something high quality that you can reproduce utilizing your Cricut machine!

The most effective method to make an immense farmhouse sign, DIY farmhouse sign, form wooden farmhouse signs

Occasion paper cut pictures are not by any means the only things you can make! In my girl's room, I cut some paper butterflies and taped to the divider like they are taking off. She delighted in those butterflies for a long time until the day we moved. I, despite everything, have the butterflies to utilize again on the off chance that she needs to… which is likewise an advantage of using paper stylistic theme… you can without much of a stretch get it together to be used some other time!

Update a young lady's room with this Girls Bedroom Decor with a Purple, Pink, and Teal Theme. This young ladies purple room stylistic layout is, for the most part, DIY room style ventures caused utilizing my Cricut To investigate, paint, cardstock, and other modest materials. We went with a Teal room subject, so it wasn't purple over-burden. We joined a Pink room topic on the grounds that our little girl had such a significant number of extra pink stylistic theme things since her past room was pink.

Froth Projects

Did you realize that Cricut can cut froth? I'll give you how pure cutting froth with Cricut Explore is underneath!

Froth Stamps

DIY froth stamps are the ideal fledgeling Cricut create! Cutting froth with Cricut was one of the first Cricut made speciality ventures I backed in 2015 (I even composed a blog entry about it here!).

Step by step instructions to make a stamp, making stamps, DIY froth stamps, cutting froth with Cricut, can Cricut cut froth, cutting froth sheets with Cricut, cutting foam with Cricut Explore, Cricut froth ventures, Cricut froth sheets, create froth stamps, how to make froth stamps, make your own stamps make froth, froth stamps kids, how to make stamps, froth stamps wooden squares.

Customized Mugs, Plates, and Jars, and More

Making Cricut Mugs, Plates, and Jars is one of my most loved Cricut Craft Projects. You can without much of a stretch update your home stylistic layout by adding a straightforward decal to existing canisters, and that's only the tip of the iceberg. In the event that you don't have plain canisters, utilize the luxuriate side!

Customized Cricut Coffee Mugs

On the off chance that you are new to utilizing Cricut machines or are keen on figuring out how to utilize your Cricut to make DIY mugs, at that point this post is for you! I incorporated a free Christmas SVG document beneath to give you some Cricut mug thoughts and guidelines on making a mug with Cricut. Making Cricut espresso Mugs is simpler than it looks! This is an enjoyment Cricut Explore Air venture that an apprentice can make.

I've for the longest time been itching to figure out how to utilize my Cricut to make DIY mugs! Cricut cup thoughts, Cricut Mugs dishwasher safe, how to make Cricut cups, Cricut vinyl on cups, Cricut espresso Mugs, How to make a Custom Mug with Cricut, How to make an espresso cup with Cricut, Cricut Explore Air ventures, making a cup with Cricut, utilizing Cricut vinyl on cups, Cricut vinyl, Cricut Christmas ventures, Cricut Christmas presents #Cricutchristmas #Cricutvinyl.

You needn't bother with a lot of vinyl to make your own mugs! I utilized extra piece vinyl to make this Clover picture for my Yeti mug for St. Patrick's Day...

Cricut ventures, Cricut Explore Air 2 Projects, Cricut Explore Air Projects, Cricut Explore Projects, free Cricut ventures, Cricut vinyl ventures, Cricut venture thoughts, Cricut Air 2 activities, Cricut machine ventures, Cricut Explore ventures for apprentices, Cricut instructional exercises for amateurs, Cricut for learners, Cricut ventures novice, Cricut ventures fledgeling texture, farmhouse Cricut ventures novice, Cricut mugs novice, DIY Cricut ventures tenderfoot, vinyl Cricut Projects

I likewise made this EASY heart picture utilizing remaining vinyl on my Yeti mug for Valentine's Day! I made a framework of heart shape for another venture and had within remaining, so I simply took advantage of my mug!

Cricut ventures, Cricut Explore Air 2 Projects, Cricut Explore Air Projects, Cricut Explore Projects, free Cricut ventures, Cricut vinyl ventures, Cricut venture thoughts, Cricut Air 2 undertakings, Cricut machine ventures, Cricut Explore ventures for novices, Cricut instructional exercises for learners, Cricut for novices, Cricut ventures amateur, Cricut ventures tenderfoot texture, farmhouse

Cricut ventures fledgeling, Cricut mugs apprentice, DIY Cricut ventures novice, vinyl Cricut Projects

Cricut Personalized Plates

This Love You More Free SVG Cut File is a charming method to amaze your darling on Valentine's Day and other sentimental festivals. Locate the free SVG, DXF, EPS, and PNG slice record beneath to make this too simple DIY! I utilized the cut document on a serving plate, a plate, and a mug, yet this would look charming on a shirt, a pack, thus significantly more!

SVG EPS DXF PNG Free cut document Love You more Valentine's Day

Cricut Personalized Soap Bottles

I customized (Rae Dunn roused) these bricklayer container cleanser holders by including my own Cricut cut vinyl. Simply include clear exchange tape (my preferred exchange tape and the contact paper is just $1 and is #11 on this rundown!)

Cricut ventures, Cricut Explore Air 2 Projects, Cricut Explore Air Projects, Cricut Explore Projects, free Cricut ventures, Cricut vinyl ventures, Cricut venture thoughts, Cricut Air 2 undertakings, Cricut machine ventures, Cricut Explore ventures for fledgelings, Cricut instructional exercises for amateurs, Cricut for novices, Cricut ventures tenderfoot, Cricut ventures learner texture, farmhouse Cricut ventures apprentice, Cricut mugs novice, DIY Cricut ventures novice, vinyl Cricut Projects

Cricut Personalized Candle Jars

I additionally customized these Dollar Tree jolts subsequent to making my own soy candles! I found the SVG structures for Sweet Pumpkin Pie and Sweater Weather at my preferred spot to discover FREE SVG documents.

Take a stab at making your own non-harmful candles utilizing soy and fundamental oils. Continue perusing to figure out How To Make Soy Candles With Essential Oils! In the event that you like Pumpkin Spice plans, pumpkin candles, and basic oils then you are going to adore making these DIY soy wax candles! This instructional exercise incorporates how many fundamental oils to add to candles, how to make soy candles with basic oils, and data on the best way to get your young living starter units! Youthful Living Essential Oils for Beginners #DIYsoycandles #younglivingessentialoils

Cricut Personalized Drink Koozies

Utilize iron-on or heat move vinyl to make some enjoyment drink koozies! I made some for my child's educators one year, and they cherished them!

This educator thankfulness blessing thought is magnificent! Who doesn't cherish koozies? Instructor end of school blessing thoughts | Cricut Explore Crafts | Cricut iron-on creates | Cricut Easy Press | educator thoughts | educator gratefulness week

Cricut Welcome Door Mat

A DIY Doormat is a Cricut venture that I've made a few times! Have you seen those amusing or customized mats on the Internet recently? Assuming this is the case, I wager you've just done your exploration to perceive the amount they cost ($25-$40 for unique request on Etsy!). These doormats are overly simple to DIY and customize with your own innovative plan (while setting aside cash), and I'll give you how!

Valentine's Day Cricut Welcome Mat

I made this Love Shack mat in the wake of hearing the melody on the radio and figured, that would make an enjoyment mat!

I love this DIY Valentine's Decor thought! Figure out how to utilize your Cricut Explore to make a DIY doormat entryway tangle, Valentine's Welcome tangle, DIY home style on a tight spending plan, DIY home stylistic theme dollar store, LOVE SHACK, mat DIY, DIY mat, customized mat, DIY custom mat.

Cricut Fall Doormat

I made a Fall mat that became a web sensation on Instagram and Cricut clients wherever needed to have a go at making their own doormat with this hack!

I love this Fall stylistic theme thought! Figure out how to utilize your Cricut Explore to make a DIY doormat entryway tangle and an adorable Fall doormat! Fall invite signs entryway patios | Fall Welcome tangle | DIY home stylistic theme on a tight spending plan | DIY home stylistic layout dollar store #fallfrontporchdecor

#falldecorideas    #fallhomedecor    #Cricutcraftideas #Cricutsvgfiles

DIY Halloween Doormat

When you begin making mats, it can turn into a compulsion! LOL! Look at this Halloween mat and incidentally, all the SVG documents to make these doormats are FREE in my computerized asset library!

Figure out how to utilize your Cricut Explore to make a DIY doormat entryway tangle and a charming Halloween doormat! Halloween invite signs entryway patios | Halloween Welcome tangle | DIY home style on a tight spending plan | DIY home stylistic layout dollar store

Farmhouse Signs

Farmhouse signs are one of my FAVORITE things to make utilizing my Cricut. I have composed a few posts about structure your own wood farmhouse signs, utilizing old wood, utilizing froth sheets and paint sticks, and repurposing freedom farmhouse signs to include your own Cricut-made decals.

Froth Board Dollar Tree Signs

These DIY Dollar Store Farmhouse Signs are going to overwhelm you! These are not your commonplace Farmhouse signs, but rather they sure appear as though them! The mystery is that all materials cost under $1 to make these signs (less the Cricut structure). I posted an image of these signs on Instagram and everybody went wild for the plain sign with the balancing wreath on it however the potential outcomes are unfathomable with including your own structure, statements, and picture to these $1 DIY signs!

You wouldn't accept these farmhouse signs are made utilizing dollar store things! DIY Farmhouse stylistic theme dollar store, DIY Dollar Store Christmas Decor, DIY Dollar Store Crafts, Dollar store DIY stylistic layout, DIY Farmhouse sign, DIY farmhouse sign Cricut, DIY farmhouse sign instructional exercise, Farmhouse style signs, DIY Christmas embellishments #dollarstorecrafts #diyfarmhousesigns #dollarstorechristmas

Wood Signs

Once in a while, I simply take a bit of scrap wood (either from old ventures or found in the piece area at stumble stores), and I paint them and include my own Cricut decal. Include a sawtooth holder the back, and you have a simple farmhouse sign! This nativity wood sign has been too famous with my perusers...

Carefully assembled Wooden Nativity Silhouette stylistic theme.

I additionally shared on Instagram how to make a FAUX wood outline utilizing scrap wood (clue: you have to recolour the sides utilizing painters tape to make a fringe, at that point use painters tape to paint within white!)

Cricut ventures, Cricut Explore Air 2 Projects, Cricut Explore Air Projects, Cricut Explore Projects, free Cricut ventures, Cricut vinyl ventures, Cricut venture thoughts, Cricut Air 2 activities, Cricut machine ventures, Cricut Explore ventures for novices, Cricut instructional exercises for apprentices, Cricut for learners, Cricut ventures amateur, Cricut ventures novice texture, farmhouse Cricut ventures tenderfoot, Cricut mugs novice, DIY Cricut ventures fledgeling, vinyl Cricut Projects

Use Dollar Tree decals for a farmhouse sign at that point include your own structure as I did with this farmhouse Unicorn sign. My adherents on Instagram went insane when they saw this Cricut/Dollar Tree hack! I utilized a Dollar Tree Unicorn Decal at that point included my own Quote (Don't Stop Believing) to the sign for a simple 5-minute craft!

I like to lessen and repurpose farmhouse signs, so I utilize the front and rear of each sign, AND once in a while, I utilize removable vinyl and update my s...

And afterwards during Christmas...

The most effective method to make a tremendous farmhouse sign, DIY farmhouse sign, form wooden farmhouse signs

Or then again this Free Hugs sign that I made for Valentine's Day...

Cricut ventures, Cricut Explore Air 2 Projects, Cricut Explore Air Projects, Cricut Explore Projects, free Cricut ventures, Cricut vinyl ventures, Cricut venture thoughts, Cricut Air 2 activities, Cricut machine ventures, Cricut Explore ventures for learners, Cricut instructional exercises for fledgelings, Cricut for amateurs, Cricut ventures apprentice, Cricut ventures novice texture, farmhouse Cricut ventures novice, Cricut mugs tenderfoot, DIY Cricut ventures novice, vinyl Cricut Projects

At that point, I changed the vinyl on that sign for Spring...

Cricut ventures, Cricut Explore Air 2 Projects, Cricut Explore Air Projects, Cricut Explore Projects, free Cricut ventures, Cricut vinyl ventures, Cricut venture thoughts, Cricut Air 2 undertakings, Cricut machine ventures, Cricut Explore ventures for fledgelings, Cricut instructional exercises for apprentices, Cricut for tenderfoots, Cricut ventures amateur, Cricut ventures novice texture, farmhouse Cricut ventures learner, Cricut mugs novice, DIY Cricut ventures novice, vinyl Cricut Projects

In the event that you need more motivation to make signs utilizing your Cricut machine, Follow Me On Instagram! I'm continually sharing a sneak look into my most recent DIY in my Instagram stories and sparing the how-to recordings as features or on my IGTV channel!

Cricut ventures, Cricut Explore Air 2 Projects, Cricut Explore Air Projects, Cricut Explore Projects, free Cricut ventures, Cricut vinyl ventures, Cricut venture thoughts, Cricut Air 2 undertakings, Cricut machine ventures, Cricut Explore ventures for amateurs, Cricut instructional exercises for apprentices, Cricut for learners, Cricut ventures tenderfoot, Cricut ventures fledgeling texture, farmhouse Cricut ventures novice, Cricut mugs novice, DIY Cricut ventures novice, vinyl Cricut Projects

Customized Pillows, Blankets, Furniture

You can customize anything with your Cricut machine utilizing Iron-On or HTV (Heat Transfer) items. I strongly prescribe the Cricut Easy Press and this HTV.

Texture Image Pillows

Consistently when the special seasons moves around, I see the occasion stylistic layout in stores and ponder internally, "I can make that." Have you seen those Fabric-cut and sewn on Pillows during Christmas, Easter, Valentine's Day, and different occasions? I at long last chose to make my own DIY Easter pad and Valentine's Day pad utilizing my Cricut machine!

Easter rabbit pennant DIY felt rabbit, Easter rabbit creates, Easter Bunny SVG, Easter rabbit printable, Easter rabbit sewing, Easter rabbit DIY, Easter rabbit style, Easter adornments, Easter stylistic theme, Dollar store Easter Decorations, farmhouse Easter stylistic theme, Easter mantle stylistic layout, do it without anyone's help Easter stylistic layout, charming DIY Easter beautifications, designs for the home, felt Easter rabbit design, texture Easter Pillow, Cricut Easter undertakings, Cricut Pillow, DIY Easter pad by means of @SMPblog

Here are two or three cushions that I made Christmas 2017 utilizing the Cricut Maker Machine, bison plaid texture, and Ikea pad covers!

Cricut ventures, Cricut Explore Air 2 Projects, Cricut Explore Air Projects, Cricut Explore Projects, free Cricut ventures, Cricut vinyl ventures, Cricut venture thoughts, Cricut Air 2 activities, Cricut machine ventures, Cricut Explore ventures for fledgelings, Cricut instructional exercises for amateurs, Cricut for novices, Cricut ventures novice, Cricut ventures novice texture, farmhouse Cricut ventures novice, Cricut mugs novice, DIY Cricut ventures learner, vinyl Cricut Projects

I picked pictures without such a large number of subtleties, so the cut was speedy and simple, similar to this snowman cushion...

Cricut ventures, Cricut Explore Air 2 Projects, Cricut Explore Air Projects, Cricut Explore Projects, free Cricut ventures, Cricut vinyl ventures, Cricut venture thoughts, Cricut Air 2 activities, Cricut machine ventures, Cricut Explore ventures for amateurs, Cricut instructional exercises for tenderfoots, Cricut for apprentices, Cricut ventures learner, Cricut ventures novice texture, farmhouse Cricut ventures fledgeling, Cricut mugs novice, DIY Cricut ventures novice, vinyl Cricut Projects

Texture Letter Pillow

I made this next texture cut cushion during Valentine's Day and during the remainder of the year, I show it in our main room (on the bed). It would make the ideal recently marry blessing as well!

#5minutecraft with Cricut Maker Projects: Cutting Fabric Letters With Cricut! bite the dust cut texture letters, removing letters of texture, texture letters, cutting texture letters with Cricut, removing letters of texture, Valentine's Day create, Valentine Crafts, DIY Valentine's Day makes, Valentines Day Crafts stylistic layout, Cricut Valentines Day Crafts

Iron-On/Heat Transfer Vinyl Pillow

This charming red truck cushion is made with heat move vinyl (this is my most loved HTV), and you can discover the SVG document to make this pad here! I sewed the edge of the cushion with red pom-pom strip for more detail.

Cricut ventures, Cricut Explore Air 2 Projects, Cricut Explore Air Projects, Cricut Explore Projects, free Cricut ventures, Cricut vinyl ventures, Cricut venture thoughts, Cricut Air 2 undertakings, Cricut machine ventures, Cricut Explore ventures for novices, Cricut instructional exercises for apprentices, Cricut for learners, Cricut ventures amateur, Cricut ventures novice texture, farmhouse Cricut ventures novice, Cricut mugs tenderfoot, DIY Cricut ventures novice, vinyl Cricut Projects

Stencilled Pillows

Prepare to be blown away. You needn't bother with HTV or texture to make pads utilizing your Cricut in light of the fact that you can likewise utilize texture paint!

One of the first Cricut ventures I made was stencilling these devoted cushions. I made a stencil utilizing substantial cardstock and Cricut, taped the paper stencil to the pad spread and painted with texture paint.

DIY devoted pads for July fourth gathering stylistic layout!

Customized Outdoor Chairs

Did I say customized seats? That's right! I needed to add my own touch to some exhausting open-air seats, so I included one of my preferred Design Bundle pictures utilizing Cricut Iron-on. These seats have been outside for 12+ months they despite everything look incredible!

DIY outside seashore pool seats

Felt Projects

The thoughts are interminable with regards to utilizing felt, and the expense is so low, why not load up on felt whenever it's on special!

Felt Bunny Banner

Making a felt pennant is one of the most straightforward apprentice Cricut extends and will refresh your regular home style without going through a huge amount of cash. Figure out how to make a felt Easter pennant underneath!

Easter rabbit standard DIY, felt rabbit, Easter rabbit makes, Easter Bunny SVG, Easter rabbit printable, Easter rabbit sewing, Easter rabbit DIY, Easter rabbit stylistic layout, Easter adornments, Easter style, Dollar store Easter Decorations, farmhouse Easter stylistic theme, Easter mantle style, do it without anyone else's help Easter stylistic theme, charming DIY Easter designs, enhancements for the home, felt Easter rabbit design, texture Easter Pillow, Cricut Easter tasks, Cricut Pillow, DIY Easter pad.

Felt Sleep Mask

In the event that you love unicorns and staying in bed, this tenderfoot Cricut rest cover venture is an enjoyable approach to utilize your Cricut Maker Machine. I get inquired as to whether the Cricut Explore can cut felt and for certain ventures, indeed, it can. Be that as it may, for an undertaking this way (with little subtleties and cuts), I suggest the Cricut Maker machine with the sharp rotating edge.

Felt Christmas Tree

I made this felt tree with adornments for my children when they were more youthful. They adored embellishing their own tree with this enjoyment and simple Cricut Christmas DIY!

DIY Cricut Felt Christmas Tree Ornaments

Felt Christmas Garland

This felt festoon with vintage Christmas lights will keep going for quite a long time to come! I utilized my Cricut Maker Machine to cut the felt, at that point sewed each light together and loaded down with polyfill. You can take a stab at making these with a paste firearm on the off chance that you wear' have a sewing machine.

Felt Flowers

I made these felt blossoms to provide for relatives on a Christmas journey. Rather than wearing coordinating shirts, I made everybody these Christmas corsages to wear on their wrist, in their hair or stuck to a coat. They were a hit!

Figure out how to make a Corsage or Boutonniere for your Christmas occasions or a sweet Christmas present! Felt blossoms, Felt Christmas Ornaments, DIY corsage wristlet, corsage wedding, clasp DIY, corsage instructional exercise, make a corsage, felt creates, felt adornments, DIY felt blossoms, Christmas Cruise outfit,

Christmas Cruise, family equips, #feltcraftideas #diycorsage

Customized Seasonal Decor and Crafts

Occasional Decor and Crafts are the most enjoyable to DIY utilizing a Cricut machine. I love making something that I found in stores for less by utilizing my Cricut machine. Here are a couple of my top picks...

Customized Ornaments

This next Cricut DIY is one of my most mainstream posts! Rae Dun motivated adornments are overly simple to make with your Cricut machine. Get some plastic adornments, add paint and Cricut decals to make these simple Cricut Christmas Craft!

These DIY Rae Dunn Christmas Ornaments were so natural to make! She utilized clear plastic decorations loaded up with paint and vinyl cut with a Cricut investigate the machine. She even has the free picture to download and the text style and size to make these Rae Dunn roused Christmas stylistic theme yourself!

Customized Pumpkins

Rae Dun propelled. Pumpkins are very simple to make with your Cricut machine. Get some Craft Pumpkins and add Cricut decals to make these simple Cricut Fall Craft!

These DIY Rae Dunn Halloween pumpkins are so natural to cause utilizing your Cricut To investigate or Silhouette Machine! Get the free SVG document now!

Customized Easter Eggs

Rae Dun propelled Easter eggs are too simple to make with your Cricut machine. Get some white speciality eggs for $1 and add Cricut decals to make these simple Cricut Easter Craft!

Cricut ventures, Cricut Explore Air 2 Projects, Cricut Explore Air Projects, Cricut Explore Projects, free Cricut ventures, Cricut vinyl ventures, Cricut venture thoughts, Cricut Air 2 undertakings, Cricut machine ventures, Cricut Explore ventures for fledgelings, Cricut instructional exercises for novices, Cricut for tenderfoots, Cricut ventures apprentice, Cricut ventures novice texture, farmhouse Cricut ventures novice, Cricut mugs amateur, DIY Cricut ventures novice, vinyl Cricut Projects

Print Then Cut Crafts

I love to print at that point cut Cricut creates on the grounds that they lessen make time definitely! Prior to the Print at that point cut element, you needed to cut all the shading cardstock expected to make something. It was so tedious to make little cupcake toppers, and so on! That is the reason I think Print at that point Cut Cricut ventures are ideal for amateurs!

Halloween Treat Holders

These Halloween treat holders are anything but difficult to make with Cricut. Simply transfer the free SVG document (get it here), follow the instructional exercise here (measuring, and so on), including treats and you, host an adorable gathering favour or Halloween treats!

These Cricut Print Then Cut DIY Halloween Treats are the ideal kindness for Halloween gatherings, and that's only the tip of the iceberg. Halloween treats for school parties, Halloween treats for kids, Halloween treat packs, Halloween treats for grown-ups, Cricut Print and Cut, Cricut Print at that point Cut, Cricut print and cut ventures, Cricut print and cut free printable, stunt or treat sacks DIY thoughts, stunt or treat sacks.

Forest Treat Holders

These forest treat holders are like the Halloween treat holders above. My companion Abbi from Abbi Kirstin assortments gives you a free record to make these Print at that point Cut forest animals utilizing Cricut!

Print at that point Cut Greeting Cards.

Make your life simpler by attempting a portion of Cricut's make-it-now Print at that point cut welcome cards whenever you're in a scramble for a welcome card!

Clothing (totes, shirts, socks, shoes)

Here are some Easy Cricut Beginner Project Ideas to make your own Apparel (totes, shirts, socks, shoes)!

Iron-On T-Shirts

I made this skull and bones St. Patrick's Day shirt for my child in 2017 and everybody cherished it, so I added a free SVG document to make it in my library! Transfer the picture, size it is relying upon the size of the T-shirt, and iron the picture. For more assistance, allude to this video!

Cricut ventures, Cricut Explore Air 2 Projects, Cricut Explore Air Projects, Cricut Explore Projects, free Cricut ventures, Cricut vinyl ventures, Cricut venture thoughts, Cricut Air 2 tasks, Cricut machine ventures, Cricut Explore ventures for fledgelings, Cricut instructional exercises for amateurs, Cricut for apprentices, Cricut ventures tenderfoot, Cricut ventures novice texture, farmhouse Cricut ventures novice, Cricut mugs learner, DIY Cricut ventures novice, vinyl Cricut Projects

In the event that You Can Read This Socks

These "In the event that you can understand this" socks are entertaining and make fix blessings. You can change the truism on the subsequent sock to state anything you desire. I've made a few of these socks and significantly offer a BUNDLE SVG document in my shop so you can make these socks in minutes and give as blessings (or use for yourself, hehe).

Cause these DIY To present to me my espresso socks matched with Starbucks espresso as an enjoyment occasion blessing thought for espresso darlings!

Cricut ventures, Cricut Explore Air 2 Projects, Cricut Explore Air Projects, Cricut Explore Projects, free Cricut ventures, Cricut vinyl ventures, Cricut venture thoughts, Cricut Air 2 tasks, Cricut machine ventures, Cricut Explore ventures for novices, Cricut instructional exercises for learners, Cricut for amateurs, Cricut ventures tenderfoot, Cricut ventures novice texture, farmhouse Cricut ventures novice, Cricut mugs fledgeling, DIY Cricut ventures apprentice, vinyl Cricut Projects

Stencilled T-Shirts/Apparel

A Cricut hack I used to do before I put resources into iron-on was to make my own stencils and paint pictures and statements on attire and clothing. This Less Monday More Summer T-shirt was stencilled utilizing texture paint!

I love the way simple this Less Monday More Summer shirt was to cause utilizing my Cricut To investigate!

I trust this post gave you a few thoughts for your Cricut Explore ventures for amateurs. Being a fledgeling utilizing Cricut, vinyl Cricut Projects, and other Cricut materials don't mean you can't attempt new things. A portion of the Cricut extends on this apprentice rundown may appear to be difficult to you right now, however, once you begin attempting a couple DIY Cricut ventures utilizing your Cricut Explore or Cricut Maker Machine, you will feel increasingly great difficult further developed Cricut Projects!

# Chapter 4:
# How to master the use of integrated "Design Space"

Is it accurate to say that you are attempting to pick up everything about Cricut Design Space and you don't have a clue where to begin?

Learning another side interest or ability can be scary from the start. I get it; now and again we don't have the foggiest idea where to begin in light of the fact that there's such a considerable amount of data out there and it's merely overpowering.

For me, the most ideal approach to learn and ace Cricut Design Space is from the earliest starting point!

When you have an away from of what each symbol and board is for, at that point, you can genuinely delve in and begin investigating further and further.

Once in a while, we rush to hop from undertaking to extend – Hey That's alright as well! BTDT – But I feel that knowing your work zone will assist you with taking your inventiveness to an unheard-of level.

The motivation behind this article is to show you and show you an outline of each Icon, and Panel of the Cricut Design Space Canvas Area.

As time goes, I will make progressively complex instructional exercises for EVERY single symbol and, or work. So on the off chance that you need to become familiar with a logo or ability, I urge you to tap the available connections.

Cricut Design Space Whats everything for

How about we learn together!

Before we delve in, how about, we realize what the Cricut Design Space Canvas Area is.

Step by step instructions to work with Iron-On - Make T-shirts.

The Cricut Design Space Canvas Area is the place the entirety of the enchantment occurs before you cut your tasks.

Configuration Space is the place you finish up and sort out your manifestations. Right now, no one but you can utilize and transfer your text styles and pictures, yet you can likewise use Cricut's top-notch images and textual styles by means of individual buys, Cricut Access, and Cartridges.

Presently, That we understood that definition off the beaten path, we should begin!

Note: If you are as yet realizing what a Cricut is and which one you ought to get; I energetically prescribe you to peruse this post where I walked you through 50+ inquiries when I got the Cricut. FYI I went through various long periods of research and an entire week to assemble this ultimate guide.

Page Content show

Beginners Cricut Design Space Canvas Tutorial – What's beginning and end for?

Putting resources into a Cricut is pointless on the off chance that you don't figure out how to ace Design Space since you will consistently require this product to cut any extend.

As I would like to think, Cricut Design Space is an astounding device for novices, and on the off chance that you have no involvement in some other Design programs like Photoshop or Illustrator, you will find that in spite of the fact that it looks overpowering, it's straightforward.

You folks, on the off chance that I can do it, you can as well!

Then again, in the event that you have review involvement in any of the Adobe Creative Cloud applications or Inkscape. You will see that this program is only a breeze. Configuration Space, it's, for the most part, to clean up your tasks and make negligible structures with Shapes and Fonts.

In the event that you need something progressively complex, you are going to require your own structures or Cricut Access. That is where you gain admittance to their supergiant library. Get familiar with it right now direct I set up.

At the point when you sign in to your Cricut Design Space record and need to begin or alter another venture, you will do every single thing from a window known as CANVAS.

Canvas Area in Cricut Design Space is the place you do the entirety of your editings before you cut your ventures.

I get it!

There are such a large number of catches, choices, and activities that you may feel lost. Try not to stress, I am here en route, perking you up and urging you to continue onward.

On this post, you are going to realize what EVERY SINGLE ICON on the Canvas region is for. To maintain everything in control and straightforward, we are going to isolate the canvas into four areas and four hues:

Top Panel Yellow – Editing Area

Left Panel Blue – Insert Area

Right Panel Purple – Layers Panel

Canvas Area Green

Tip: This is anything but a short post, so I urge you to get some espresso with certain doughnuts or treats if conceivable.

Cricut Design Space partitioned in 4 hues.

Prepared to vanquish Cricut Design Space?

Top Panel Cricut Design Space

The top board in the Design Space Canvas zone is for altering and masterminding components on the canvas zone. From this board, you can pick what sort of text style you'd prefer to utilize; you can change sizes, adjust plans, and then some!

This board is isolated into two sub-boards. The first permits you to spare, name, lastly cut your ventures. Also, the subsequent one will empower you to control and alter things on the canvas zone.

Sub-board #1 Name Your Project and Cut it

This sub-board permits you to explore from the Canvas to your profile, activities, and it additionally sends your finished ventures to cut.

Top Panel Cricut Design Space

Sub-board #1

Top Panel Toggle Cricut Design Space

Switch Menu

At the point when you click on this catch, another entire menu will slide open. This menu is a convenient one. However, it's not part of the Canvas, and that is the reason I won't be going into a great deal of detail.

Fundamentally, from here, you can go to your profile and change your photograph.

There are other valuable and specialized things you can do from this menu like aligning your machine, edges; likewise refreshing the Firmware – Software – of your gadget.

You can likewise deal with your memberships from Cricut Access, your record subtleties, and that's just the beginning.

I prescribe you to tap on each connection with the goal that you investigate everything that Cricut Design Space has for you.

Note: On the settings alternative, you can change the perceivability and estimations of the Canvas; this is clarified better toward the finish of this post when I explain about the canvas territory.

Venture Name

All ventures start with an *Untitled "title," you can just name a task from the canvas territory after you've set at any rate one component (Image, shape, and so on.).

My Projects

At the point when you click on my ventures, you will be diverted to your library of things you have just made; this is extraordinary on the grounds that occasionally you may need to re-cut a formerly made task. Along these lines, there's no requirement for you to reproduce a similar venture again and again.

Spare

This choice will initiate after you've set one component on your canvas territory. I suggest you spare your task as you go. Despite the fact that the product is on the cloud, if your program crashes, there goes your difficult work with it!

Producer – Explore (Machine)

Drop-down menu machine determination Cricut Design Space

Contingent upon the kind of machine you have you should choose either the Cricut Joy, Maker or the Cricut Explore Machine; this is significant in light of the fact that on the Cricut Maker you will discover choices that are just accessible to that specific machine.

Along these lines, in the event that you have a Maker and you are structuring with the Explore alternative ON you won't have the option to initiate the devices that are for the creator.

The various alternatives are for line type. (I will cover on this instructional exercise)

Make it

At the point when you are finished transferring your documents and prepared to cut snap-on Make it!

Down underneath, there's a screen capture of what you would see. Your ventures are separated by mats as per the shades of your undertaking.

From this window, you can likewise build the number of ventures to cut; this is incredible in the event that you are anticipating making more than one cut.

At the point when you click on to make it. This is the thing that you see.

At the point when you click on Make it. This is the thing that you see.

Subpanel #2 – Editing Menu

It's precious, and it will assist you with editing, orchestrate, and compose text styles and pictures on the Canvas Area.

Top Panel – Editing Menu

a. Fix and Redo

Some of the time while we work, we commit errors. These little fastens are an extraordinary method to address them.

Snap Undo when you make something you don't care for, or commit an error. Snap Redo when you incidentally erase something you would not like to delete or adjust.

(On the off chance that just there were something comparable forever itself lol)

b. Linetype and Fill

This choice will mention to your machine what instruments and cutting edges you are going to utilize.

Remember that relying upon the machine you have chosen on the highest point of the window (Maker or Explore), you will have various choices.

Linetype

This alternative will tell your machine when you are cutting your venture, what instrument you will utilize. At the present time, there are seven choices (Cut, Draw, Score, Engrave, Deboss, Wave, Perf).

In the event that you have a Cricut Maker, all alternatives will be accessible, however on the off chance that you have an Explore you will just have the Cut, Draw, and the Score choice.

Here is a more top to bottom clarification of each apparatus.

Cut

Except if you transferred a JPEG or PNG picture to the Canvas; "Cut" is the default line type that the entirety of your components on your canvas will have; this implies when you press MAKE IT, your machine will cut those plans.

With the Cut choice chose, you can change the fill of your components, by the day's end, this deciphers in the various shades of materials you will utilize when you cut your ventures.

On the off chance that you need assistance with finding out about the Cricut Blades and the distinctions, I prescribe you this ultimate guide and instructional exercise I set up. It's the best on the web, much the same as this instructional exercise.

Draw

In the event that you need to compose on your structures, you can do it with your Cricut!

At the point when you relegate this line type, you will be incited to pick any of the Cricut Pens you have (You need explicit pens, except if you host a third get-together connector). At the point when you select a specific structure, the layers on your canvas region will be sketched out with the shade of the pen you picked.

With this apparatus, when you click Make it, rather than cutting, your Cricut will compose or draw. Note: This alternative DOESN'T shading your structures.

Score

The score is an increasingly energetic rendition of the Scoring line situated on the left board. At the point when you relegate this credit to a layer, the entirety of the structures will show up scored or ran.

Now, when you click on Make it. Your Cricut won't cut, yet it will score your materials.

For these kinds of activities, you will require the scoring stylus or the scoring wheel. Notwithstanding, remember The wheel just works with the Cricut Maker.

On the off chance that you have questions about what materials you need, I recommend you read this article. It's a definitive guide for you to realize what embellishments and materials you genuinely need.

## Etch, Deboss, Wave, and Perf (New)

These are the most up to date devices that Cricut has discharged for the Cricut Maker machine, and with them, you will have the option to make stunning consequences for various kinds of materials.

They typically work with the Quick Swap Adaptive Tool, so on the off chance that you as of now have one, you can purchase the tips.

I don't have these apparatuses yet in light of the fact that they will be turning out in two or three weeks, yet once I have them on my hands, I will give you a quick update.

## Fill

The fill alternative is, for the most part, to be utilized for printing and examples.

It might be initiated when you have Cut as a "line type." No Fill implies that you won't print anything.

Print is by a long shot, probably the best element Cricut has on the grounds that it permits you to print your structures and afterwards cut them; this is breathtaking, and indeed, it's what spurred me to get a Cricut in any case.

I structure vast amounts of printables for kiddos and grown-ups, and for taking photographs – for my presents – I had on cut each and every seemingly insignificant detail!

Ahhhgggg, I genuinely needed to cry inevitably. I am a lefty, and scissors truly make my hands hurt. So the Cricut is a really big lifesaver for me.

Anyway, we are returning to the Printing alternative. At the point when this Fill choice is dynamic after you click Make it; first, you'll send your records to your home printer and afterwards have your Cricut do all the hard work. (Cutting)

Another excellent alternative for the Print Type is Patterns!!! You folks, this is so cool. Utilize Cricut's decisions, or transfer your own; you can add an example to virtually any sort of layer.

The creative mind is your cutoff!

Suppose it's Valentine's Day. You can make a beautiful card with a previously made example from Cricut Access (Membership, not free), or your own. At that point, print and cut simultaneously.

Alter your examples to meet your requirements!

Much obliged to you, Cricut!

c. Select All

At the point when you have to move the entirety of your components inside the canvas zone, you may battle to choose them individually.

Snap Select all to choose the entirety of the components from the canvas.

d. Alter

Top Panel Edit Cricut Design Space

This symbol will permit you to cut (expel from the canvas), (duplicate a similar thing, leave unique unblemished), and glue (embed replicated or reduce components on the canvas territory) stuff from the canvas.

The Edit Icon has a drop-down menu.

The cut and duplicate alternative will be actuated when you use have a determination of at least one components from the canvas zone. The Paste choice will be empowered once you duplicate or cut something.

e. Adjust

In the event that you have reviews involvement in other visual computerization programs, in all probability, you'll realize how to utilize this menu.

On the off chance that you aren't acquainted with the Align Tools, let me reveal to you something; the Align Menu is something that you need to ace to flawlessness.

I will do a full instructional exercise for this, however, while it turns out; this is what each adjust work implies:

Adjust: This capacity permits you to adjust the entirety of your structures, and it's actuated while choosing at least two components.

— Align Left: When utilizing this setting, the entirety of the components will be adjusted to one side. The farthest part to one side will direct where the whole of different parts will move towards.

— Center Horizontal: This choice will adjust your components on a flat plane; this will entirely focus on content and pictures.

— Align Right: When utilizing this setting, the entirety of your components will be adjusted to one side. The uttermost part to the correct will direct where the whole of different elements will move.

— Align Top: This alternative will adjust the entirety of your chose plans to the top. The farthest component to the top will direct where the entirety of different components will move.

– Center Vertically: This choice will adjust your components vertically. It's helpful when you are working with sections, and you need them composed and adjusted.

– Align Bottom: This choice will adjust the entirety of your chose plans to the base. The uttermost component to the base will direct where the entirety of different components will move.

– Center: This alternative is an extremely cool one. At the point when you click on "focus," you are focusing, both vertically and evenly, one structure against another; this is especially valuable when you need to focus content with a shape like a square or a star.

Disseminate: If you need a similar separating between components, it's very tedious to do everything all alone, and it's not 100% right. The disseminate catch will assist you with an excursion with that. For it to be actuated, you should have at any rate three components chose.

– Distribute Horizontally: This catch will convey the components on a level plane. The uttermost left and right plans will decide the length of the dispersion; this implies the things that are in the middle will be conveyed between the most far off left and right structures.

– Distribute Vertically: This catch will disperse the components vertically. The uttermost top and base plans will decide the length of the dispersion; this implies the things that are in the inside will be appropriated between the most far off top and base structures.

Adjust in Cricut Design Space

Step by step instructions to adjust in Cricut Design Space

f. Mastermind

Top Panel Arrange Cricut Design Space

At the point when you work with different pictures, content, and structures, the new manifestations you add to the canvas will consistently be before everything. In any case, a portion of the components of your structure should be in the back or front.

With the orchestrate alternative, you can compose the components no problem at all.

Something incredible about this capacity is that the program will realize what thing is on the front or back and, and when you select it, Design space will initiate the accessible alternatives for that specific component. Cool right?

These are the choices you get:

– Send to back: This will move the chose component right to the back.

– Move Backward: This choice will move chosen the thing only one stage back. So in the event that you have a three-component structure. It will resemble the cheddar in a cheddar sandwich.

– Move Forward: This alternative will move the component only one stage forward. Ordinarily, you would utilize this choice when you have at least four things you have to sort out.

– Sent to front: This alternative will move the chose component right to the front.

g. Flip

Top Panel Flip Cricut Design Space

On the off chance that you have to mirror any of your structures in Cricut Design Space, this is an extraordinary method to do it.

There are 2 choices:

— Flip Horizontal: This will mirror your picture or structure evenly. Similar to a mirror; It's helpful when you are attempting to make a left and right plans. Model: You are constructing a few wings, and as of now have the left side; with Flip, you can reorder the left-wing, and presto! Presently you have both (left and right) wings!

— Flip Vertical: This will flip your structures vertically. Sort of like you would see your appearance on the water. In the event that you need to make a shadow impact, this choice would be extraordinary for you.

h. Size

All that you make or type in Cricut Design Space has a size. You can alter the size from the component in self (when you click on it). In any case, on the off chance that you need a thing to have an accurate estimation, this choice will permit you to do as such.

Something basic is the little lock. At the point when you increment or decrease the size of a picture, the extents are constantly bolted. By tapping on the little lock, you are telling the program that you would prefer not to keep similar measurements.

I. Turn

Much the same as size, pivoting a component is something you can do rapidly from the canvas territory. Notwithstanding, a few structures should be turned on a particular point. On the off chance that that is the situation for you, I prescribe you to utilize this capacity. Else, you will invest such a lot of energy battling to get a component calculated the manner in which you need it to be.

j. position

This crate gives you where your things are on the canvas zone when you click on a particular structure.

You can move your components around by determining where you need that component to be situated on the canvas zones. It's convenient; however, it's a further developed instrument.

By and by, I don't utilize it that much since I can show signs of improvement with the arrangement instruments I referenced previously.

k. Text style

At the point when you click on this board, you can choose any text style you need to use for your undertakings. You can channel them and quest for them on the highest point of the window.

On the off chance that you have Cricut Access, you can utilize any of the considerable numbers of text styles that have somewhat green A toward the start of the textual style title.

In any case, on the off chance that you don't have Cricut get to, Make sure you utilize your framework's textual styles; else you will be charged when you send your venture to cut.

l. Style

When you pick your text style, you have the choice to change its structure.

A portion of the alternatives available:

– Regular: is the default setting, and it won't change the presence of your textual style.

– Bold: it will make the textual style thicker.

– Italic: it will tilt the textual style to one side.

– Bold italic: it will make the textual style thicker and tilt to one side.

m. Text dimension, Letter and Line Space

Top Panel Font Spacing and size Cricut Design Space

I can't communicate enough about how AMAZING these choices are. Particularly the letter dividing.

Text dimension: You can transform it physically from here. I normally simply alter the size of my text styles from the canvas territory.

Letter Space: Some text styles have an impressive hole between each letter. This alternative will permit you to decrease the space between letters rapidly. It's truly a distinct advantage.

Line Space: this choice will handle the space between lines in a section; this is exceptionally helpful in light of the fact that occasionally I am compelled to make a solitary line of content since I am not content with the dividing between lines.

n. Arrangement

This Alignment varies from the other "arrangement" I clarified previously. This alternative is for passages.

These are the alternatives you have:

– Left: Align a section to one side

– Center: Align a passage to the middle

– Right: Align a passage to one side.

o. Bend

Top Panel Curve Cricut Design Space

This choice will permit you to get extra innovative with your content!

With this capacity, you can bend your content — the most ideal approach to get familiar with it's by playing with the little slider.

At the point when you move the slider to one side, it will bend the content upwards; and when you move it to one side, it will twist the content inwards.

Note: on the off chance that you move the slider totally to one side, or right; you will shape a hover with your textual styles.

p. Advance

Top Panel Advanced Cricut Design Space

Advance is the keep going alternative on the altering board.

Try not to be threatened by the name of this drop-down menu. When you realize what the entirety of the choices is for, you will see they are not so difficult to utilize.

– Ungroup to Letters: This choice will permit you to isolate each letter, into a solitary layer (I will clarify progressively about Layers down underneath); utilize this, in the event that you have plans to adjust each and every character.

– Ungroup to Lines: This choice is outstanding, and it will permit you to isolate a section on singular lines. Type your passage, at that point, click on ungroup to lines, and there you have it; a different line that you would now be able to adjust.

– Ungroup to Layers: This one is the trickiest of these alternatives. This choice is just accessible for Multi-Layer text styles; these sorts of textual styles are only available for single buys and, or Cricut Access.

A multi-layer text style is a sort of textual form that has more than one layer; these text styles are extraordinary on the off chance that you need to have some shadow or shading around it.

Imagine a scenario where you like a textual style that is multi-layer, and you don't need the additional layer. Simply select your content and afterwards click on ungroup to layers to isolate each and every segment.

Figure out how to Edit Text in Cricut Design Space

A fast interruption to welcome you over on my Instagram! Label me and let me see the entirety of your beautiful manifestations. I am so glad when I see individuals are utilizing my instructional exercises!

Left Panel – Insert Shapes, Images and More

Left Panel Cricut Design Space

Left Panel

With the top board (that I just disclosed to detail) you will alter the entirety of your plans.

In any case, where do they all originate from? They all originate from the Cricut Design Space Left Panel.

This board is tied in with embeddings shapes, pictures, prepared to cut tasks, and that's only the tip of the iceberg. From here you are going to include everything you are going to cut.

This board has seven alternatives:

– New: to make and supplant another task in the canvas zone.

– Templates: this permits you to have a guide on the sorts of things you are going to cut. Suppose you need to press on vinyl on a onesie. At the point when you select the layout, you can structure and perceive how the plan would resemble.

– Projects: Add prepared to cut undertakings from Cricut Access.

– Images: Pick single pictures from Cricut Access, and cartridges to make an undertaking.

– Text: Click here to include content your canvas region.

– Shapes: Insert a wide range of forms on the canvas.

– Uploads: Upload your pictures and slice records to the program.

There's something essential that you have to consider on this board; except if you have Cricut Access, Cricut Images, prepared to cut undertakings, and Cricut textual styles cost cash. In the event that you use them, you should pay before you cut your task.

In the event that you, despite everything, have questions about Cricut Access. Help yourself out and read this ultimate guide I set up for you to see if you need it or not. It's truly a lifeline.

Presently, we saw a little preview of what everything was for on this board. How about we see what happens when you click on every one of those catches.

a. New

At the point when you click on NEW, and in the event that you are as of now dealing with a venture, you will get an admonition on the window asking you whether you need to supplant your task or not.

If you need to supplant your task, make a point to spare all the progressions from the present undertaking; else, you will lose such challenging work. After you save, a new and void canvas will open up for you to begin.

Cricut Design Space Canvas Left Panel new-1

b. Formats

Formats help you to imagine and perceive how your task will fit on a specific surface. I think this component is simply out of this world.

On the off chance that you need to customize style things, this device is grand since you can choose sizes and various kinds of apparel. Furthermore, they additionally have a ton of different classes that you can browse.

In the event that you need to get the hang of everything increasingly about formats and how to utilize them, I prescribe you are perusing this post.

Note: layouts are for you to picture. Nothing will be cut when you get done with structuring and send your venture to be cut.

c. Ventures

On the off chance that you wish to remove right, at that point Projects is the place you need to go! When you select your task, you can modify it; or snap-on make it, and adhere to the cutting guidelines.

Tip: Most of the ventures are accessible for Cricut Access individuals, or you can buy them as you go. Notwithstanding, there are a bunch of undertakings, FREE for you to cut contingent upon the machine you have. Simply look to the base of the classes' drop-down menu and select the gadget you claim.

No reasons!

Cricut Design Space Canvas Left Panel ventures

d. Pictures

Pictures are impeccable when you are assembling your own undertakings; with them, you can include an additional touch and character to your artworks.

You can look by watchwords, classifications, or cartridges.

Cartridges are a lot of pictures that you have to buy independently; some of them accompany Cricut Access, and some not. (Brands, for example, Disney, Sesame Street, Hello Kitty, and so on are not part of Cricut Acces)

Cricut has FREE pictures to cut each week. You can discover them when you click on Categories.

Cricut Design Space Canvas Left Panel pictures 1

e. Content

Whenever you need to type on the Canvas Area you should tap on Text; at that point, a little window that says Add message here will open on the canvas.

Figure out how to alter content like a professional on this incredible guide I set up!

f. Shapes

Cricut Design Space Canvas Left Panel shapes

Having the option to utilize shapes, it's essential! With them, you can make straightforward and less muddled, and (furthermore) excellent tasks.

There're nine shapes you can browse:

— Square

— Triangle

— Pentagon

— Hexagon

— Star

— Octagon

— Heart

The last alternative isn't a shape, yet a remarkable and incredible asset called Score Line. With this alternative, you can make overlap and score your materials.

On the off chance that you need to make boxes or love everything about card making, the Score Line will be your closest companion!

Figure out how to alter shapes like a Pro!

g. Transfer

Last, however, not least!

With this choice, you can transfer your records and pictures. The web is loaded up with them; there are vast amounts of bloggers that make extends for nothing.

Gracious! What's more, to make sure you know, I likewise have a FREE developing library with vast amounts of printables and SVG records fit to be cut.

I would cherish for you to have the option to gain admittance to every one of them. It's 100% Free for my daydreamers (otherwise known as endorsers) look at a live review here, or get access here.

Note: The transfers you see on the picture directly down underneath are inside my phenomenal library!

Right Panel – Learn All about Layers

To set you up for progress and before I disclose to you what each symbol is about on the Layers Panel, let me give you a little presentation of what a layer is.

Layers speak to each and every component or plan that is on the canvas zone.

Consider it like apparel; when you get dressed, you have various layers that make up your outfit; and relying upon the day, or season, your gear can be primary or elaborate.

Along these lines, for a freezing day, your layers would be clothing, pants, shirt, coat, sock, boots, gloves, and so on.; and for a day at the pool, you would just have one layer, a Swim Suit!

The equivalent occurs with a plan; contingent upon the multifaceted nature of the undertaking you are dealing with, you'll have various sorts of layers that will make up your whole venture.

For instance, we should imagine that you are structuring a Christmas Card.

What might this card have?

Possibly a content that says Merry Christmas, a tree, the card itself, maybe an envelope also?

My point is that the entirety of the little plans and components that are a piece of that undertaking are layered.

A few layers can be adjusted; however, different layers, like JPEG and PNG pictures, can't; this is a direct result of the idea of the document or the sheet itself.

For example, a book layer can be changed over into different sorts of layers; at the same time, when you do that, you'll lose the capacity to alter that content.

As you go, you will get familiar with what can or can't do with layers.

I trust that gave you a smart thought of what a layer is! Presently how about we realize what each and every symbol is for on this correct board.

a. Gathering, Ungroup, Duplicate and Delete

These settings will make your life simple while moving things around the canvas territory, so make a point to mess with them.

Gathering: Click here to aggregate layers. This setting is convenient when you have various layers that make up an unpredictable plan.

Suppose you are chipping away at an elephant. In all probability (and if this is an SVG or cut record) the elephant will be made out of various layers (the body, eyes, legs, trunk, and so forth.); If you need to join, additional shapes, and content; in all likelihood is that you will be moving your elephant over the canvas region a ton.

In this manner, by gathering the entirety of the elephant layers, you can ensure that everything will remain sort out and nothing will escape place when you move them around then canvas.

Ungroup: This alternative will ungroup any assembled layers you select on the canvas region or layers board. Utilize this choice in the event that you have to alter (size, kind of text style, and so on.) a specific component or layer from the gathering.

Copy: This choice will copy any layers or plans you have chosen on the layers board or canvas.

Erase: This alternative will erase any components you have chosen on the canvas or layers board.

b. Linetype/Fill

Each thing on the Layers Panel will show what Linetype or Fill you are utilizing (Cut, Write, Score, Perf, Wavy, Print, and so on.).

c. Layer Visibility

The little eye that shows up on each layer on the layers board speaks to the visibility of a plan. At the point when you are uncertain about whether a component looks excellent, rather than erasing it, click on the little eye to shroud that structure. Note: When you wrap a thing, the eye will have a cross imprint.

Tip: By tapping on a layer and hauling it, you can move a specific plan on top or under; you could state that this works like the Arrange choice (sent to the front, back, and so forth.).

d. Clear Canvas

This "layer" permits you to change the shade of your canvas; in the event that you are attempting to perceive how a specific plan looks with an alternate shading. The intensity of this setting is released when you use it alongside the Templates apparatus since you can alter the shading and the alternatives of the layout itself.

e. Cut, Weld, Attach, Flatten and Contour

These apparatuses you see here are unimaginably significant! So ensure you ace them to flawlessness. I won't go into a lot of detail on them since they merit instructional exercises all alone.

Be that as it may, I will give you a short clarification of what they are about by utilizing the realistic down underneath.

Cut, Weld, Attach, Flatten, and Contour Info-Graphic

As should be evident in the realistic, the first plan is a pink circle and a greenish-blue square. Presently we should perceive what happens when I utilize these choices.

Cut

The cut apparatus is ideal for removing shapes, content, and different components, from various plans.

At the point when I chose the two shapes and tapped on the cut, you can see that the first document got all cut up; to give you what the ultimate result was, I reordered the "cut outcome" and afterwards isolated the entirety of the pieces that came about because of cutting.

Become familiar with the cut apparatus

Weld

The welding instrument permits you to consolidate at least two shapes in one.

At the point when I chose the two shapes and tapped on Weld, you can see that I made a totally different shape. The shading is dictated by the layer that is on the back, that is the reason the new form is pink in shading.

Append

Append works like gathering layers. However, it's all the more impressive.

At the point when I chose the two shapes and tapped on append, you can see that the layers simply changed shading (controlled by the layer that is on the back). In any case, the shapes are associated, and this connection will stay set up, much after I send my undertaking to be cut.

Get familiar with Weld and Attach.

Level

This apparatus is additional help for the print at that point Cut Fill setting; when you change the fill from no fill to print, that applies to only one layer. In any case, imagine a scenario where you wish to do it to numerous shapes at that point.

At the point when you are finished with your structure, select the layers you need to print altogether, and afterwards click on straighten.

At the point when you are finished with your planned (you can't switch this in the wake of leaving your undertaking), select the layers you need to print altogether, and afterwards, click on the level.

Right now, component turned into a print at that point cut plan, and that is the reason it isn't demonstrating a dark edge (where the side will experience) any longer.

Get familiar with Flatten and Print at that point Cut.

Shape

Shape Cricut Design Space Example

The Contour instrument permits you to conceal undesirable bits of a plan, and it might be actuated when a shape or configuration has components that can be forgotten about.

For this model, I joined the first structure fit as a fiddle with the welding apparatus; at that point, I composed in the word form and cut it against the new shape, and utilized the Contour instrument to conceal the internal circles of the two letters O and the inward piece of the letter R.

Get familiar with the shaping instrument.

f. Shading Sync

Shading Sync is the last alternative of the layers board.

Each shading on your canvas region speaks to an alternate material shading. On the off chance that your plan has numerous shades of yellows or blues; would you say you are sure you need them?

In the event that you just need one shade of yellow, similar to this model. Simply snap and drag the tone you need to dispose of and drop it on the one you need to keep.

Canvas Area

The canvas territory is the place you see the entirety of your structures and components. It's incredibly natural and easy to utilize!

Cricut Design Space Canvas Area

a. Canvas Grid and Measurements

The canvas territory is isolated by a framework; this is extraordinary on the grounds that each and every square you see on the Grid causes you to envision the cutting mat. At last, this will assist you with maximizing your space.

You can change the estimations from creeps to cm and turn the matrix on and off when you click on the top board flip and afterwards select Settings. (You can see this switch menu, directly in the start of this instructional exercise)

A window will spring up with the entirety of the choices.

Configuration Space Settings For turning framework now and again

Turn the Grid now and again.

b. Determination

Whenever you select at least one layers, the choice is blue, and you can change it from the entirety of the four corners.

The "red x" is for erasing the layers. The right upper corner will permit you to pivot the picture (despite the fact that on the off chance that you need a particular point, I prescribe you to utilize the turning device on the altering menu).

The lower right catch of the choice, "the little lock," keeps the size corresponding when you increment or lessening the size of your layer. By tapping on it, you are presently ready to have various extents.

c. Zoom In and Out

To wrap things up. On the off chance that you need to find in a more enormous or littler scope (without adjusting the actual size of your plans), you can do it by squeezing the "+ and - " signs on the lower-left corner of the canvas.

That is it – You are not an amateur any longer!

I trust this instructional exercise was helpful for you! On the off chance that you read it and examined it intentionally, let me disclose to you something that you are not a fledgeling.

You have graduated!

# Chapter 5:
# How to work with vinyl

There are a couple of fundamental strides in working with cement vinyl, and we will experience everyone. They are setting up your cut document, cutting, weeding, and applying. That is it! For exhibit purposes, I will make a DIY vinyl decal to add to my iPad case. I am utilizing my "Creators Gonna Make" structure that you can get over in my So Fontsy shop.

Stage ONE – PREP CUT FILE

The initial phase in the making with vinyl is to set up your cut document in the cutting machine programming you are utilizing. (On the off chance that you don't have an electronic cutting machine like a Silhouette or Cricut, you can cut vinyl by hand. However, it merely is increasingly hard to get unpredictable structures. Look at this DIY grower I enlivened with vinyl cut totally by hand for a model.)

WHAT'S A CUT FILE?

At the point when I state "cut record," I mean the plan that you need to cut from vinyl and put on your shirt or other surfaces. The most widely recognized cut record type is presumably SVG, yet you may be utilizing a.Studio, .png, .dxf, or .jpg document contingent upon the product you are utilizing. I, for one, am a devotee of SVG records since they work with most cutting programming. (NOTE: You should have at Silhouette Studio Designer Edition or higher to utilize SVG documents, and I certainly prescribe that Silhouette clients move up to Silhouette Studio Designer Edition.)

WHERE TO FIND CUT FILES

On the off chance that you are searching for cut documents, at that point, make sure to look at the free cut records I have here on the blog. I likewise have a cut record shop and take an interest in a month to month cut document group that you might need to look at. At last, I am likewise consistently sticking marvellous sliced documents to my Silhouette board here.

For this model, I am utilizing my Makers Gonna Make cut record structure, which is accessible in my shop.

SCALE DESIGN

When you have your structure and surface selected, you have to gauge your surface to decide how large you should cut the plan.

measure for situation of a DIY vinyl decal

I will typically simply snatch a ruler or measuring tape to decide how enormous I need my decal to be. I chose I needed it to be around 6 inches wide.

Open up your cut document structure in your cutting machine programming, and afterwards scale the plan to the size you need. I am utilizing Silhouette Studio programming, yet the procedure ought to be comparative with any program you are using. Just snap on the structure and afterwards drag the corner handle to scale the plan to the size you need.

A Beginner's Guide to Cutting and Applying Vinyl Decals

2. CUT DESIGN FROM VINYL

Presently we are prepared to stack our vinyl into the cutting machine.

Spot VINYL ON CUTTING MAT

It is conceivable to cut vinyl straightforwardly from the move without a tangle utilizing your Silhouette, and I will include a post about how to do that soon, however, for the present, allows simply centre around how to cut with a cutting mat. You can get Silhouette Cameo cutting mats in 12" x 12" and 12" x 24". The Cricut cutting mats are extremely comparative, and I have utilized Cricut mats with my Silhouette.

Whatever tangle and machine you are utilizing, put your glue vinyl paper backing side down onto your knot, so the hued vinyl side is looking up (see picture beneath). If your vinyl went ahead of a move, you could remove a piece to fit on your tangle. For my decal, I chose to utilize Expressions Vinyl Series 31 removable vinyl in Bright Berry. (For more data on the best way to pick the correct vinyl for your venture, look at this post.)

put vinyl on cutting mat

Change CUT SETTINGS AND CUT

At last, you should modify the cut settings in your product or on your machine to work with the material you are utilizing. This procedure will be somewhat unique for each cutting machine, however simply make a point to pick the settings for the specific sort of vinyl you are utilizing (sparkle vinyl may require unexpected settings in comparison to customary lustrous vinyl, for example). Working with my Silhouette, I chose Vinyl, Matte from the Materials menu.

material settings for cutting cement vinyl in outline studio

I prescribe doing a little test cut, mainly when you are working with another material to ensure the cut settings will function admirably with the content you are utilizing before endeavouring to cut the whole structure. You need the edge to slice through the vinyl neatly without slicing through the support. This is known as a "kiss cut," and it will make it a lot simpler to weed and apply your decal in the following stages. On the off chance that your test slice has experienced the paper backing, you may need to diminish your thickness/profundity or cutting edge setting, or if the test cut didn't go entirely through the vinyl, you might need to build the thickness/profundity or edge setting.

At the point when you are content with your cut settings, load your cutting mat with the vinyl paper throwing in the towel into your machine, and cut!

cutting vinyl with outline appearance

3. Get rid of EXCESS VINYL

The subsequent stage is classified as "weeding." Basically, weeding just methods expelling any abundance vinyl from around your structure that you would prefer not to be moved to your last item.

Step by step instructions to AVOID WASTING VINYL WHEN WEEDING

On the off chance that your cut structure is significantly littler than the bit of vinyl, you cut it from, at that point I prescribe first cutting off the excess vinyl before weeding. You can simply utilize a couple of scissors and trim around your plan. This permits you to use the remainder of your vinyl piece for another undertaking. (In my weeding pictures underneath, I really cut a square shape around my structure with my Silhouette first and afterwards cut off the extra vinyl with scissors after weeding. Whichever way works!)

TIPS FOR WEEDING ADHESIVE VINYL

To weed off the overabundance vinyl, you will require a device. I for one use, love, and suggest this weeding snare. It is sharp and works extraordinary for evacuating that vinyl. You can likewise utilize a Silhouette snare, a Cricut snare, tweezers, an art blade, or even a straight pin.

If you have any trouble seeing your cut lines, you can attempt delicately bowing your vinyl or holding it up to a light or window. The Cricut Bright Pad is another choice. When you locate your cut lines, utilize your snare or other weeding instruments to delicately lift up the edge of the negative space and remove it up from the paper backing. I like to begin by expelling the vinyl from around my plan first and afterwards expel the pieces from inside letters and different sections of the design. how to weed cement vinyl

3. USE TRANSFER TAPE TO APPLY DECAL

Since you have your plan all weeded, you will have a lot of independent bits of vinyl situated on your paper sponsorship, and you have to move them from the paper support to your outermost surface. To do this effectively and keep all however pieces where they should be, you need to move tape or move paper. (I have likewise composed a full bit by bit direct about working with move tape that you can look at directly here.)

Folks – a decent exchange tape is your distinct advantage in turning into a DIY vinyl decal ace. There are bunches of various brands and kinds of move tape accessible, yet I genuinely like utilizing and strongly suggest one of the clear exchange tapes from Expressions Vinyl. One of the rolls will last you until the end of time. On the off chance that you get it, I don't figure you will lament that buy.

APPLY TRANSFER TAPE

Whatever move tape you use, start by removing a piece about the size of your decal, and smoothing it on to the highest point of your decal.

apply move tape to glue vinyl

Utilize an application apparatus, scrubber instrument, or even an old Mastercard to smooth the exchange tape onto the decal. Next, gradually strip the exchange tape and the vinyl decal up off of the paper backing.

pull up DIY vinyl decal

APPLY VINYL DECAL

At that point, cautiously position your decal over your surface. Tenderly spot one end down superficially and smooth it out with your fingers. At that point, utilize your application or scrubber instrument to shine the decal onto your surface. Keep in mind, the vinyl's cement is actuated through weight, so give it a decent rub to get it to stick well.

The most effective method to apply DIY vinyl decal cut with outline appearance

At last, strip off your exchange tape, and you are completely done! Your great DIY vinyl decal is applied!

Since you realize how to utilize glue vinyl to make a basic vinyl decal, you should evaluate some further developed cement vinyl systems:

Figure out how to make multi-hued vinyl decals effectively with enrollment marks.

Figure out how to utilize the pivot strategy for exact application and smooth application on bent surfaces.

Figure out how to make bright and point by point vinyl stickers with printable cement vinyl.

Part 12: How to utilize the Cricut simple push on iron-on vinyl

My learner's manual for working with glue vinyl will walk you through the entirety of the fundamental strides of slicing and applying cement vinyl to make your own fantastic vinyl decals.

Next up, Heat Transfer Vinyl!

Step by step instructions to USE HEAT TRANSFER VINYL

On the off chance that you have for a long while been itching to make your own proficient looking shirts, home-style, and that's only the tip of the iceberg, at that point, you must take a stab at creating with heat move vinyl.

Instructions to utilize heat move vinyl for tenderfoots

This present tenderfoot's manual for iron-on vinyl will walk you through the entirety of the essential strides of making your own vinyl shirts.

MORE VINYL CRAFTING TECHNIQUES

On the off chance that you are hoping to give a shot considerably more vinyl creating systems and venture thoughts, don't miss these:

Figure out how to make multi-hued vinyl decals effectively with enlistment marks.

Make sense of how to use the rotate strategy for precise application and smooth application on bent surfaces.

Figure out how to make beautiful and itemized vinyl stickers with printable cement vinyl.

Become familiar with the knockout system for layering heat move vinyl without additional thickness.

Figure out how to apply heat move vinyl to wood.

Figure out how to apply heat move vinyl to calfskin.

Figure out how to apply HTV to shoes.

I trust this asset assists with kicking you off with vinyl making. I love working with vinyl, and I believe you will as well!

# Chapter 6:
# Simple projects with vinyl and card stock

Simple CRICUT PROJECTS FOR BEGINNERS

This post and the photographs inside it might contain Amazon, or other offshoot joins. On the off chance that you buy something through the connection, I may get a little commission at no additional charge to you.

New to utilising your Cricut? These simple Cricut ventures for learners are the ideal spot to begin! Consider going all in with this enjoyment yet straightforward Cricut creates utilising your Cricut Explore Air 2 or Cricut Maker machine.

New to utilising your Cricut? These simple Cricut ventures for tenderfoots are the ideal spot to begin! Consider making the plunge with this enjoyment however basic Cricut makes utilising your Cricut Explore Air 2 or Cricut Maker machine.

Getting your Cricut out of the crate and begin making with it very well may be threatening to anybody! Your Cricut Maker or Cricut Explore Air 2 can appear such a convoluted machine, with such a significant number of edges, mats, materials and instruments. Fortunately, I have two bits of uplifting news for you!

I've gathered together a lot of Cricut ventures for fledgelings right now! These ventures are ideal for figuring out how to utilise your machine, just as the edges, mats, devices, and materials you might need to mess with.

(Furthermore, on the off chance that you need to learn much progressively about your Cricut, look at the full Cricut Academy! It will help you absolutely vanquish your Cricut!)

It will be ideal if you pin from unique sources.

Simple CRICUT PROJECTS FOR BEGINNERS

Simple IRON ON VINYL PROJECTS

The most effective method to Make a T-Shirt with the Cricut

One of the most essential Cricut materials is iron-on vinyl, additionally called heat move vinyl (or HTV for short). Look at my How to Use Cricut Iron-On Vinyl post. It has everything (and I mean the world!) you would ever need to know.

The most evident decision is utilising it on attire. Look at my Using Iron On Vinyl on a Shirt post for tips on picking vinyl, getting it arranged, and ensuring it sticks—for good!

At that point investigate these other iron-on vinyl extends that is overly straightforward for apprentices!

Iron-on Vinyl on a Wood Sign

"Don't Moose With Me" Infant Onesie

Making a Banner with Iron-on Vinyl on Card Stock

Sprinkle Shoes

Adaptable Tooth Fairy Pouches

Simple ADHESIVE VINYL PROJECTS

Send the children to class, sports practices and day camp with their own one of a kind customised water bottles! They are anything but difficult to make utilising your Cricut, and the children will cherish having something only for them.

Glue Vinyl is another material that is incredible for novice Cricut clients. It's fundamentally a major sticker! My Easy Personalized Water Bottles are an enjoyment venture. You can likewise look at my manual for Using Transfer Tape, just as Layering Adhesive Vinyl.

Here's some cement vinyl extends that even the freshest Cricut client can make!

DIY Pantry Labels

Wood Sign with Adhesive Vinyl

Utilising Adhesive Vinyl on an Ornament

Sprinkle Halloween Pumpkin

Simple CARD STOCK + PAPER PROJECTS

Get the SVG slice records to make these moving organiser bookmarks on your Cricut or other cutting machines! Also, get nine other persuasive cut records right now Fresh Cuts pack.

Card stock and paper are my two preferred materials for new Cricut clients since they are so economical—flawless when you're beginning and would prefer not to go through a ton of cash! I love making a wide range of things, similar to these Inspirational Planner Bookmarks!

Need to make more paper and card stock Cricut ventures for tenderfoots? Look at these fan top choices from my blog:

Hogwarts House Bookmarks

DIY Easter Jars

Simple Layered Mother's Day Card

Halloween Bat Place Cards

Mammoth Paper Snowflakes

MORE CRICUT PROJECTS FOR BEGINNERS!

Searching for considerably more tenderfoot Cricut makes? Look at these enjoyment thoughts from a portion of my preferred bloggers! These specialities are, for the most part, great in case you're simply beginning utilising your Cricut Explore or Cricut Maker.

Iron-On Vinyl: Easy Christmas Tea Towels

Iron-On Vinyl: DIY Pool Float Koozies

Iron-On Vinyl: Straightforward I Love You, Gift Tag, With Cricut from 100 Directions

Iron-On Vinyl: DIY "Mama Is On A Break" Socks from Realistically Functional

Iron-On Vinyl: "Fries Before Guys" Top by Pretty Providence

Iron-On Vinyl: 10-Minute Perfect Heart Shirt by Hello Creative Family

Designed Iron-On Vinyl: Cricut Patterned Iron-On Cactus Shirt from See Vanessa Craft

Cement Vinyl: Easy DIY Sign from Ginger Snap Crafts

Cement Vinyl: Customise Phone Case

Cardstock: DIY Ice-Cream Card from Inspiration Made Easy

Cardstock: Straightforward DIY Fiesta Inspired Cake Toppers and Treat Bags from The Crafted Sparrow

Cricut Iron-On Designs: Mermaid Pillow by Our Crafty Mom

Cowhide: DIY Leather Key Fob Gift Idea With Cricut from Lydi Out Loud

Texture: Heart Shaped Fabric Coasters Using the Cricut Maker from Create and Babble

New to utilising your Cricut? These simple Cricut ventures for tenderfoots are the ideal spot to begin! Consider making the plunge with this enjoyment yet basic Cricut creates utilising your Cricut Explore Air 2 or Cricut Maker machine.

MAKE EVEN MORE WITH YOUR CRICUT

Purchase THE CRICUT OF YOUR DREAMS!

Cricut creator

# Chapter 7:
# Instruction to upload images with a Cricut machine

If you have a fresh out of the plastic new Cricut, look at these other extraordinary posts that will help acquaint you with your new machine! Furthermore, look at my Cricut venture exhibition for huge amounts of Cricut venture thoughts!

What Is A Cricut Machine and What Can I Do With It?

Step by step instructions to Set Up A Brand New Cricut Maker and Do Your First Project!

What Materials Can A Cricut Machine Cut? Here Are Over 100!

Instructions to Cut Vinyl With A Cricut Machine: A Step By Step Guide

How Do I Upload My Own Images With A Cricut Machine?

Having the option to transfer your own pictures gives you huge amounts of opportunity to make anything you need with your Cricut. You can transfer anything from straightforward, level jpeg pictures too complex multi-layer vector records and Cricut Design Space will naturally process them so you can print, cut, decorate, or use them any way you need in your Cricut venture!

To transfer any picture to Cricut Design Space, first, open Cricut Design Space in your internet browser. Snap the green "New Project" button in the upper right-hand corner to make a clear venture.

At the base of the toolbar on the left half of the task is a "Transfer" symbol. Snap that to open the Upload tab.

step by step instructions to transfer my own picture with a Cricut machine

From here you can transfer either a fundamental picture (a solitary layer picture, for example, .jpg, .gif, .bmp, or .png) or a vector picture (a multi-layer picture, for example, .svg or .dxf).

instructions to transfer my own picture with a Cricut machine

I made a basic realistic in Adobe Illustrator and spared it as both a jpg and an SVG document so I can tell you the best way to transfer a fundamental picture and a vector picture to Cricut Design Space.

JPEG and SVG record prepared to transfer to Cricut Design Space

Step by step instructions to transfer a fundamental picture to Cricut Design Space.

Most pictures you see on the web are fundamental pictures, implying that they are level, single-layer pictures. They can have numerous hues and even have all the earmarks of being 3D. However, the real picture itself is made with pixels of various hues to give the presence of concealing or profundity. These single-layer pictures can be made in programs like Adobe Photoshop, PicMonkey, Canva, and other straightforward photograph altering programming. Photographs from your telephone or camera are additionally essential, level pictures.

You can transfer .jpg, .gif, .bmp, and .png records to Cricut Design Space and they will all be transferred as a solitary layer.

Here's the way to transfer a fundamental picture. From the Upload tab in Cricut Design Space, click the green and white "Transfer Image" button.

At that point either simplified a picture record into the window or snap the green and white "Peruse" catch to open a picture document.

the most effective method to transfer my own picture with a Cricut machine

When you pick an essential picture to transfer, it will show a see on the left side and request that you select the picture type. You can look over:

Basic: a too essential picture with high-differentiate hues and either a straightforward or single-shading foundation

Reasonably Complex: a picture with certain subtleties and numerous hues, yet there is still acceptable differentiation between the subject of the picture and the foundation

Complex: an itemized picture with mixed hues or concealing/slope (these pictures are somewhat harder to work with due to the degree of detail)

For this model, I picked "Basic" since it's a basic plan. At that point, click the green "Proceed" button.

Instructions to transfer a fundamental jpeg picture to Cricut Design Space

The subsequent stage is to "process" the picture to ensure just the parts you really need to cut out make it into your task. You have three essential apparatuses you can use to process the picture:

Select and Erase: This resembles the enchantment wand instrument in PhotoShop; it permits you to choose a region or explicit shading in your transferred picture and eradicate it. On the off chance that you click the "Propelled Options" button, you can change the resilience.

Delete: This is only a standard eraser instrument. You can change the size of your eraser utilizing the slider on the left.

Harvest: You can trim away whole territories of your picture utilizing the yield device.

I use "Select and Erase" for about 90% of the pictures I transfer to Cricut Design Space; it's extremely groundbreaking and truly shrewd! For this model, I tapped on the foundation of the picture, and it eradicated the whole foundation!

Harvest and delete undesirable pieces of a fundamental jpeg picture subsequent to transferring to Cricut Design Space

I kept clicking in each star to eradicate the foundation from the stars, and afterwards, I was finished. When you have deleted all pieces of the picture that you don't need to cut out, click the green "Proceed" button.

The following stage is to choose what kind of picture you have and give it a name. You can spare your transferred picture as a Print and Cut picture, or similarly as Cut picture. In the event that your unique picture has subtleties in it (like a photograph of your children that you need to print first, at that point cut, or something where the hues are significant), spare it as Print and Cut. In the event that it is only a shape that you need to remove, you can spare it as a Cut picture.

Transfer essential jpeg picture to Cricut then spare as Print And Cut or simply Cut

Give your picture a name and include labels on the off chance that you need, at that point click the green "Spare" button.

Your transferred picture will show up in the Recently Uploaded Images area at the base of the Upload tab. Simply select your transferred picture and snap the green "Addition Images" catch to add it to your undertaking!

instructions to transfer my own picture with a Cricut machine

The most effective method to transfer a vector picture to Cricut Design Space

Vector pictures are picture documents with numerous layers, as a rule, made in a program like Adobe Illustrator. Right now, the left flap of the heart with the stars is one layer so I can remove it of blue material, and the stripes are part into two layers. Each and every other stripe is in one layer, so it tends to be removed from red material, and different stripes are a different layer so they can be removed from white material.

You can transfer .svg and .dxf documents to Cricut Design Space, and they will all be transferred as different layers with each picture layer or shading being isolated into discrete layers in Design Space.

Here's the way to transfer a vector picture. From the Upload tab in Cricut Design Space, click the green and white "Transfer Image" button.

At that point either simplified a picture document into the window or snap the green and white "Peruse" catch to open a picture record.

Since vector picture records contain the entirety of the picture subtleties inside the document itself, Cricut Design Space can really process these pictures for you consequently without you expecting to do anything!

Step by step instructions to transfer an SVG document to Cricut Design Space.

You will see a preview of your picture on the left, and after it's transferred preview layer or shading will be its own layer.

Simply give your picture a name and include labels on the off chance that you wish, at that point click the green "Spare" button.

Select your transferred picture from the Recently Uploaded Images area, at that point click the green "Supplement Images" catch to add it to your undertaking!

Transfer pictures to Cricut and afterwards embed them into your venture.

You'll see that when you embed a fundamental picture, it will show up in the dark as the heart on the left, yet the vector picture will show up in whatever hues were utilized in the first vector record. The fundamental picture will be one single layer in the Layers toolbar on the right. However, the vector picture will be part of layers or hues.

You can see that the hued heart is one layer. However, each "shape" is consequently concealed in one of three hues (red, white, and blue). In Cricut Design Space, various hues go about as "layers", so when you go to cut this plan, it will consequently part red, white, blue, and dark into four unique "cuts" with the goal that you can remove them of various hues or materials on the off chance that you wish. In the event that the SVG record you transfer is every one of the one shadings, Cricut Design Space will rather consequently part each layer into a different layer/bunch in your undertaking.

Transfer a jpeg or SVG record to Cricut Design Space

Vector pictures are much progressively incredible on the off chance that you are intending to cut various hues or materials in light of the fact that the layers naturally convert into layers in Cricut Design Space. Be that as it may, for basic cut or Print and Cut tasks, transferring an essential picture will work fine and dandy!

# Chapter 8: How to make stickers

Instructions to MAKE STICKERS WITH YOUR CRICUT +FREE STICKER LAYOUT TEMPLATES

Not exclusively will I show you how to make your stickers without any preparation, yet I will likewise give you six unique sorts of formats that will assist you with building and make the most staggering stickers on the planet.

Cricut Maker and Explore with three distinctive sticker sheets

How about we make these stickers together!

Before we go into a bit by bit instructional exercise I need to give you a little see of the things I will cover for you on this article (I don't need you to get lost).

Print at that point Cut: the alternative in Cricut Design Space that permits you to cut your stickers.

Diagram of your machine determinations and size cutoff points.

Bit by bit instructional exercise How to Make Stickers inside Cricut Design Space.

Instances of how to utilize the Free Templates I gave you to Make Stickers.

I am certain that If you follow this instructional exercise to the tee, you will be engaged to make stickers whenever, for any event.

It is safe to say that you are prepared?

How about we Daydream Into Reality?

Tip: If you see there's something that doesn't exactly appear to be identical in the product screen captures (trust me I am striving to transform them) if it's not too much trouble look at my Stay fully informed regarding Cricut Design Space article so you recognize what transforms you have to remember.

What is Print at that point Cut and how can it identify with stickers?

Print at that point Cut is the alternative in Cricut Design Space that permits you to print your plans and afterward cut them with your machine.

There are two different ways to advise your machine to Print at that point Cut. The first is by changing the Fill to Print and choosing your shading or example. The subsequent one is by straightening the layers with the Flatten apparatus situated toward the finish of the layers board.

For best practices and zero disappointments don't stress over this during your plan procedure, it will just worry you.

Simply include your shapes, content, pictures, and toward the end, level the entire thing. (I will give you this in the bit by bit instructional exercise)

Note: Although I spread a few subjects of Print at that point Cut on this article; remember that this device is an extremely hearty one. Along these lines, in the event that you need to become familiar with all there's to think about it, feel free to peruse my Print Then Cut Ultimate Guide.

Yellow Square sticker made with Cricut

## Machine and Settings for Making Cricut Stickers

There are two things you need consistently to ensure when making stickers with your Cricut.

The first is the size. You can just Print at that point Cut plans that are up to 9.25 x 6.75in. So check the size before you send your undertaking to cut, or you will get an admonition saying the picture is excessively enormous.

The other thing that you have to consider is your machine's confinements:

On the off chance that you have a Cricut Maker, you can utilize hued paper (that is not very occupied) and polished white materials.

On the off chance that you have an Explore machine, you have to utilize white paper with matte completions.

The most effective method to creator stickers with your Cricut (Maker/Explore)

Bit by bit Tutorial/Make Stickers with your Cricut

Since you know your machine necessities, it's the ideal opportunity for you to figure out how to make stickers.

Materials

Cricut Maker/Explore

Sticker Paper

Printer

Fine Point Blade

Light Grip Mat (blue)

Note: I ordinarily love Cricut's items. Be that as it may, their sticker paper is extremely thick and stalled out in my printer (I have a HP 4520 Printer) thus, on the off chance that you haven't purchased your sticker paper, I prescribe you to purchase the Silhouette Brand.

Outline sticker paper versus Cricut Printable sticker paper

In the event that you as of now have the Cricut Sticker paper, take a stab at sparing the Print and take it to Staples or Office Depot, for them to print it. Or on the other hand if that is an excessive amount of issue get the other one.

Time is cash!

Making a Methodology

Since you can utilize content, pictures, shapes, and essentially anything in Design Space to make stickers, you may get overpowered and don't where to begin.

In this way, for you to have a wonderful involvement in making stickers, I've built up a "frustrationproof" strategy.

These are the means we will follow:

Make a format (By including shapes)

Include Color or Patterns

Include content and Images

Check the estimate and Flatten

Cut your stickers

At the point when you follow this request, you can focus and spotlight on one stage at that point, and that, my companion is ground-breaking!

Note: Save your task as you go. It's very tedious and Cricut doesn't have back up alternatives.

Stage 1 - Create a Sticker Sheet Layout

Since Cricut Design Space just permits us to Print at that point Cut in a size no greater than 9.25 x 6.75in. I prescribe you to include a rule so you are constantly mindful of your space and can make a Sticker Sheet Layout.

Cricut Design Space Screenshot: Add a square shape to make a rule for your sticker sheet

Include a 9.25 x 6.75in square shape to use as a guide

To include the rule, click on the shapes button situated on the left of the canvas and select the square choice. At that point (while choosing the square) go to the alter menu on the canvas and snap the little square in the center to open extents. (we will utilize this term all through this instructional exercise)

At that point on W (width) type in 6.75 and, on H (stature) type in 9.25. Subsequent to resizing the square, change the linetype shading for white, so it's simpler for you to have a superior thought of your plan.

Note: Check out my how-to alter shapes If you feel mistook for altering the extents, and so forth.

Cricut Design Space Screenshot: Add the shapes you need to use for making the stickers.

Case of the entirety of the shapes you can use for your stickers

In the wake of making your guide, include the shapes you need for your stickers. Cricut has nine distinct alternatives for you to look over. For this instructional exercise, I utilized squares, hearts, circles, and triangles.

What we have to do now is fill our guide with a wide range of various shapes. Remember to open extents so you can make a wide range of square shapes.

Cricut Design Space Screenshot: adjust stickers so they are all together

Tip 1: Use the adjust alternative to keep your shapes and the various shapes you're adding to your sticker design sorted out. Select the components you need to adjust, and relying upon how you need to adjust them utilize the various choices.

As a rule, you will utilize Center and Distribute on a level plane or Vertically. Along these lines, Give it an attempt! You will commit a few errors while you become accustomed to it, yet once you get its hang, you won't return.

Tip 2: Create various figures for your stickers. Look at the accompanying picture for a bit by bit process.

Cricut Design Space Screenshot: bit by bit on the best way to add various components to the Cricut sheet

Stage 1: Add a square shape and triangle (you should turn the triangle so it's topsy turvy)

Stage 2: Place triangle toward the finish of the square shape. They should cover (only an indent).

Stage 3: Select the two shapes and weld to make another component for our stickers. (Weld is situated at base of the Layers board)

Stage 4: Rotate to accommodate your sticker design

Cricut Design Space Screenshot: Complete sticker page with the entirety of the shapes and erase rule

Keep including shapes in various sizes and let your creative mind fly! Your stickers will be so charming toward the end.

At the point when your design is finished, you need to erase or shroud your guide. Kindly remember to do this. Something else, your stickers won't cut after you level.

Presently, select the entirety of the shapes and change the linetype shading for white; this will permit you to have an all the more away from of what you will do straightaway.

Stage 2 - Add Colors and Patterns

It's a great opportunity to add shading to your stickers!

As I referenced above, don't stress over linetype or Print at that point Cut. We will cover that later. To add shading to your sticker, you can pick a strong foundation or a Pattern.

Add a Solid Color to your Stickers

Select the component you need to add shading to and change the shading box beside the linetype setting, situated at the top board of the canvas territory.

In the event that you click on cutting edge, you will have the option to see a more extensive range of hues, and you can likewise utilize a code to locate a particular shading.

Cricut Design Space Screenshot: add hues to your stickers

Add shading to your stickers!

Tip: To change the shade of numerous shapes simultaneously, press Shift on your console (consistently) and click on the entirety of the components you need to alter; this additionally works with designs.

Adding Patterns to Cricut Stickers

Patters are foundations you can use for your stickers or other Print at that point Cut undertakings. There are many them for you to look over.

Cricut used to charge for them, however they are free for the present, so exploit them.

Cricut Design Space Screenshot: add examples to your stickers

Investigate Patterns for your Cricut Stickers

On the off chance that you need to include designs, change the fill of the shapes you need to change for Print and afterward click on the shading box for this alternative and pick Pattern for Print Type.

You will discover numerous examples to browse. Since they don't have a code I can't show which I one utilized; So, you'll have to look down until you discover it.

At the point when you discover the example you need to utilize, try to investigate the altering alternatives of it also.

Cricut Design Space Screenshot: Edit the manner in which your example looks on your stickers

At times, Patterns will look extremely little; along these lines, more often than not, I alter them. The things I as a rule change are the scale and flat position. As you alter a Pattern, you will see the entirety of the progressions on a little see.

Stage 3 - Add Text and Images

To include content, click on the Text button situated on the left board of the canvas. In the event that you don't have a clue how to alter message in Cricut Design Space, try to peruse my instructional exercise on this theme.

When you are finished adding hues and examples to your stickers feel free to type in the content you need to utilize.

Cricut Design Space Screenshot: add content to your stickers

Add the content you need to use for your stickers

Here are a few thoughts for various sorts of sticker sheets:

Content for Planner Stickers: To-Do/Due/Get it Done/Days of week/Notes/Don't overlook/Important/Break/Appointment... and so forth

Content for relaxation stickers: Beach Day/Break/Party/Vacation/Snowboard Day/Date Night/Ocean Vibes/Enjoy life/Brunch/Girls Night Out... and so forth

What I love about making Cricut Stickers is that you can customize the content to accommodate your preferences and life when all is said in done, and that is something you could always be unable to get or purchase in a customary store.

In the wake of composing in your content, place it on the shapes you need them to be.

Cricut Design Space Screenshot: place message on your stickers and include mores shapes for differentiate

Don't they look astonishing?

Tip: If required, add more shapes to include differentiate between the examples and content.

Presently it's an ideal opportunity to add pictures to your stickers! (Snap on the Images button situated on the left board of the canvas)

Cricut Design Space Screenshot: add free Cricut pictures to your stickers

Utilize the channel to discover free pictures

You can include your own pictures, or you can likewise utilize a few pictures Cricut's Library. They do have an enrollment yet on the off chance that you like free stuff as much as I do, channel pictures and select:

My Images (check the ones you've transferred to the product)

Free (Some are in every case free, different ones are just free for a particular time)

Bought (your machine accompanies a lot of free pictures)

These are the pictures I utilized (I don't have the foggiest idea whether they will be free when you attempt to track). To discover them, glue the code in the pursuit pictures box.

Cricut Design Space Screenshot: pictures chose to add to your stickers.

Add pictures to the canvas

I prescribe you embeddings one at that point and afterward resizing it in such a case that you include them all simultaneously, your canvas will be a wreck!

Remember that when you work with pictures, once in a while they are assembled, and have various hues and sizes. So you should ungroup them to alter the hues and size of each and every component.

You may likewise need to change the extents to fit them in your sticker sheets.

Stage 4 - Check Size and Flatten

Look at how I utilized the pictures to fill the remainder of my sticker sheet. Presently we are going to get into some genuine stuff!

Note: If you despite everything have the GUIDELINE we utilized toward the starting YOU HAVE TO DELETE IT!

At the point when you complete your stickers, select all that you have on the canvas (that makes some portion of the sticker sheet) and snap on the level choice situated at the base of the Layers board.

Cricut Design Space Screenshot: Flatten all components before cutting the stickers

Remember to smooth

As should be obvious in the screen capture down underneath, our stickers look so vastly different.

Everything is on a solitary layer, and the sharp edge will experience all the layouts of each shape.

Sticker sheet subsequent to utilizing the level instrument in Cricut Design Space

Straighten Result

At the point when you are prepared to cut, click on the Make it Button situated at the upper right corner.

At long last!

How about we cut these cuties.

Stage 5 - Print and Cut your Cricut Stickers

The accompanying screen capture is the view that you'll have when you start the cutting procedure.

We utilized all the space! - Sticker paper is very costly, so make every last trace of it tally.

Outline of the Mat before cutting the stickers

Snap on Continue to choose materials

Look at everything glances set up and hit proceed. (This is the means by which you have to put the printed duplicate on your Mat)

To start with, we have to send our undertaking to the printer, so click on Send to Printer (leave all the default settings on) and afterward on Print.

Cautioning: Make sure you print on the correct side of the Sticker Paper. On the off chance that you aren't sure what side of the paper your printer prints, utilize a customary bit of paper with a blemish on it to discover.

Send your stickers to print, set the materials and burden instruments and tangle.

Print your Sticker Sheet and burden Mats and instruments

After you Print, it's the ideal opportunity for you to choose the sticker paper you are working with.

In the event that you have a Cricut Maker, peruse all materials and type in "sticker" to limit the pursuit. I picked Sticker Paper, Removable on the grounds that I didn't utilize Cricut's image.

On the off chance that you have a Cricut Explore, move the brilliant set dial on your Cricut Machine and afterward peruse materials on configuration space and pick the sticker paper you are working with.

Presently how about we move to genuine photographs!

Burden Mat with the printed sticker sheet and burden it to your Cricut machineLoad Mat

Empty the tangle from your Cricut when you are done cuttingUnload Mat

Expel stickers from the Cricut MatRemove from Mat

In the wake of choosing materials, introduce Fine Point Blade and spot the as of now Printed Sticker Paper on your Mat, load it to your machine and press the blazing Go button on your gadget.

Witness the enchantment before your eyes!

At the point when Design Space illuminates you that the cut is finished dump your Mat for the Cricut lastly expel sticker sheet from the Mat.

Stickers sheet made with the Cricut Maker

Cricut Pens composing on the stickers

There you have it! Wonderful stickers you can use for your arranging exercises.

Cricut Sticker - Get it done

Cricut Sticker - You are my jam

Cricut Sticker - Make dreams occur

Utilizing Layout Templates to Make Cricut Stickers

On the off chance that you've been perusing my site, you realize I love tossing additional treats and SVG records to make your life simpler.

Here I have six unique formats you can use for your undertakings. To get to them click on the yellow catches, at that point spare them to your PC and transfer them to Cricut Design Space.

They as of now have hues, yet don't hesitate to utilize the strategies I indicated you above to customize them anyway you need!

I won't spread again a bit by bit instructional exercise on how I did the following ones, however I will tell you the best way to transfer them and utilize these layouts in Cricut Design Space.

My motivation with these records is to give you additional assets and thoughts to work with, so you don't feel scared and need to pull out all the stops!

Goodness! Furthermore, to make sure you know, I additionally have a FREE developing library with huge amounts of printables and SVG records fit to be cut.

I would adore for you to have the option to gain admittance to every one of them. It's 100% Free for my daydreamers (otherwise known as supporters) look at a live see here, or get access here.

Transfer Sticker Templates to Cricut Design Space

To transfer your task, sign in to Cricut Design Space, and snap on to the Upload button situated on the layers board. Next, click on "Transfer Image" and select it from your PC.

Instructions to transfer sticker layouts to Cricut Design Space

Transfer Sticker Layouts to Design Space

Once transferred, the format will be under as of late transferred pictures. Select it and snap on embed pictures.

These layouts are measured effectively, so you don't need to stress over that. To alter each and every shape all alone, you have to choose the record and snap on Ungroup (situated at the highest point of the Layers board).

Sticker Sheet format in Cricut Design Space (ungroup)

Ungroup so you can alter each shape

In the event that you notice, there is a surprising shape there. To add content to it follow the means I show you in the screen capture directly down beneath.

Add content to wavy shapes in Design Space

Add content to wavy shapes

Presently look at this!

Do you perceive how unique it looks? I utilized various hues and pictures to make an alternate vibe.

This one is a greater amount of sea shore and mermaid style stickers.

Sea shore and mermaid style stickers made with Cricut.

Change hues and give the format an alternate vibe

Furthermore, just on the off chance that you are interested these are the codes of the pictures and hues I utilized:

Sea shore Style stickers printed and cut with Cricut

Sticker on a diary

You can likewise make an entire page of a similar shape. These are ideal for denoting your diaries, or in the event that you have children, you can utilize them as a prize framework.

Circle stickers format with basic shapes.

Is it safe to say that they aren't so excellent?

I utilized the circles' format layout and essential shapes to put on them.

I love the delightful way dynamic and wonderful they look. Wouldn't you concur?

Close admire the Cricut stickers made with Cricut

Full sticker sheet made with Cricut

Circle Stickers made with Cricut

To wrap things up, I need to tell you the best way to utilize format that just has squares on it.

I truly love the wonderful way It wound up!

For this sticker sheet, I chose to just utilize designs for the foundation, and Free (at that point) Cricut Images. You can utilize your statements or content also.

Utilizing examples and pictures ONLY in Cricut Design Space for making stickers model.

Examples don't have a code, so you would need to look to discover them (sorry). Be that as it may, here are following pictures I utilized:

Pick You/half worn out half charming square stickers

full sheet of Cricut stickers made with the square shape design

Cricut Explore Air 2 cutting stickers

These last ones turned out so extraordinary. Pictures don't do it equity.

I figure this kind of stickers can function as a present for a companion or somebody you love. You can likewise include empowering phrases, and so on.!

What do you think?

Well done You are a Pro at Making Cricut stickers.

# Chapter 9: Cricut scrapbooking

To start with, I open up Design Space on Cricut.com and snap on "include new structure".

Items that I use:

Cricut Maker

Cricut Deluxe Paper, Sherbet

Cricut Divine Peonies Deluxe Paper

Tombow Mono Permanent Adhesive

Second-hand shop Frame Upcycle with Chalk Couture

STEPS TO USING CRICUT DESIGN SPACE FOR SCRAPBOOKING:

Stage ONE

Assemble your photographs and commending paper for your page. Open a clear 12 x 12 canvas in Design Space.

steps to utilizing Cricut Design Space to make scrapbook pages

Stage TWO

Utilizing "shapes", embed relating shapes that are the size of the photographs you will use on your page. Change the shade of these to the shade of cardstock that you will use for tangling. (You should trim your photographs a bit)

step by step instructions to utilize Cricut configuration space for scrapbooking

Stage THREE

Supplement more shapes and pictures to fill the page. Change the shades of these to relate with the cardstock or paper that you will utilize.

The most effective method to utilize Cricut configuration space for scrapbooking

Stage FOUR

Cut out, wanted shapes and allude back to your canvas in Design Space for the situation.

Make little word labels by composing conclusions on white cardstock or vellum, at that point cutting.

Stage FIVE

Include embellishments and diary.

That "sweet dreams" plan is from Cricut, and I decided to remove it of dark vinyl rather than paper.

I trust this article makes you consider how you can utilize Cricut Design Space to assist you with making excellent scrapbook pages. In the first place, I open up Design Space on Cricut.com and snap on "include new structure".

{FTC disclaimer: I got a few things in the post complimentary. However, the sentiments are mine all mine! This post contains subsidiary connections which imply I may make a commission on the off chance that you buy something – at no extra expense to you.}

Pause! Let me show you right now, and afterwards, you can peruse progressively about my procedure in the wake of viewing:

Items that I use:

Cricut Maker

Cricut Deluxe Paper, Sherbet

Cricut Divine Peonies Deluxe Paper

Tombow Mono Permanent Adhesive

Second-hand shop Frame Upcycle with Chalk Couture

STEPS TO USING CRICUT DESIGN SPACE FOR SCRAPBOOKING:

Stage ONE

Accumulate your photographs and praising paper for your page. Open a clear 12 x 12 canvas in Design Space.

Steps to utilizing Cricut Design Space to make scrapbook pages

## Stage TWO

Utilizing "shapes", embed relating shapes that are the size of the photographs you will use on your page. Change the shade of these to the shade of cardstock that you will use for tangling. (You should trim your photographs a bit)

step by step instructions to utilize Cricut configuration space for scrapbooking

## Stage THREE

Supplement more shapes and pictures to fill the page. Change the shades of these to relate with the cardstock or paper that you will utilize.

step by step instructions to utilize Cricut configuration space for scrapbooking

## Stage FOUR

Cut out wanted shapes and allude back to your canvas in Design Space for the position.

The most effective method to utilize Cricut configuration space for scrapbooking

step by step instructions to utilize Cricut configuration space for scrapbooking

instructions to utilize Cricut configuration space for scrapbooking

Make little word labels by composing notions on white cardstock or vellum, at that point cutting.

step by step instructions to utilize Cricut configuration space for scrapbooking

Stage FIVE

Include embellishments and diary.

step by step instructions to utilize Cricut configuration space for scrapbooking

step by step instructions to utilize Cricut configuration space for scrapbooking

That "sweet dreams" structure is from Cricut, and I decided to remove it of dark vinyl rather than paper.

I trust this article makes you consider how you can utilize Cricut Design Space to assist you with making delightful scrapbook pages.

# Chapter 10:
# How to choose a new Cricut machine (powerful tips for how to buy a Cricut machine)

Along these lines, you need to purchase a Cricut. Be that as it may, you're looking on the web, and there are such vast numbers of choices! They all appear to be identical. However, they have various names like Air, One, Air 2 and Maker. What's the distinction between every one of these machines, and which device is the best choice?

Cricut Explore Machines correlation

One of the initial inquiries that individuals pose to me about the Cricut is – "Which Cricut Explore would it be a good idea for me to purchase?"

There are a couple of components to consider when you are picking which Cricut Explore machine to purchase. What's more, presently, there's even another kind of device that is one stage over the "Investigate" family — the Cricut Maker. The Cricut Maker isn't actually a Cricut Explore machine, yet I think of it as fundamentally the same as so I'll be gathering them all in the inquiry "which Cricut would it be a good idea for me to purchase?"

Today I needed to go over the likenesses and contrasts between every one of the machines and ideally help answer this famous inquiry.

Likenesses

Allows the first discussion about the highlights of the Cricut Explore and Cricut Maker that ALL of the machines share practically speaking. Regardless of which device you settle on, they all can do the accompanying:

Cut, Write, and Score

All machines can Cut, Write, and Score. The thing that matters is that a few devices do this across the board step, while others do this in two stages. We will get into that later. The fundamental thought is that all Cricut Explores and the Cricut Maker permit you to Cut out tasks and Write on them or Score them.

Simple Calligraphy utilizing the Cricut Explore pen connector! Bit by bit guidelines here! I Love the delightful way this looks!!!

>> How to Make Modern Calligraphy Art <<

Cut Many Different Materials

All machines permit you to cut a wide range of materials. On the Cricut Explore machines, there exists a Smart Dial where you can choose the material that you need to cut. There is likewise a custom setting, which permits you to look over a wide range of stuff on your PC to cut.

The Cricut Maker does not have a Smart Dial. Instead, you select every materials for cutting from your PC.

Step by step instructions to make a comfortable fall pad utilizing the Cricut Explore. Full instructional exercise for creating a cushion using Craftables heat move vinyl and a FREE downloadable cut document!

Structure Software

All machines work with Cricut Design Space. Cricut Design Space is an online programming device that permits you to configuration activities to remove utilizing your Cricut Explore. As of late, Cricut has refreshed their Cricut Design Space programming to adaptation 3. The new form is significantly quicker, and I believe it's more natural than previously.

She tells you bit by bit the best way to make a flag utilizing the Cricut Explore! Such a simple instructional exercise with incredible data!

Above: Cricut Design Space Version 2

Step by step instructions to make a comfortable fall cushion utilizing the Cricut Explore. Full instructional exercise for creating a cushion using Craftables heat move vinyl and a FREE downloadable cut document!

Transfer Your own Images for Free

All machines permit you to transfer your own pictures into Cricut Design Space and cut them out for nothing!

All machines can make Print at that point Cut structures. These are structures that can be printed out utilizing your home printer and afterwards cut out using the Cricut Explore or Cricut Maker.

She tells you bit by bit the best way to make beautiful marks utilizing the Cricut Explore! Such a simple instructional exercise with incredible data!

Contrasts

Presently we should discuss what makes these machines extraordinary and what that implies for you when choosing which one to buy.

Remote cutting utilizing Bluetooth

A portion of the machines can associate with Cricut Design Space on your PC or iPad remotely utilizing Bluetooth. The Cricut Explore Air 2, Cricut Explore Air, and the Cricut Maker all have this capacity. The the Cricut Explore OneCricut Explore Original and don't have this capacity incorporated with the machine. In any case, you can purchase a different Bluetooth Adapter for these two machines that will give them the remote cutting capacity.

Double Adapters

One element of specific machines is the double connector that takes into account both a sharp edge lodging and extra lodging to be appended simultaneously. With this dual connector, the machine can both Cut and Write or Score in a similar advance with no mediation from you. The Cricut Explore Original, Cricut Explore Air 2, the Cricut Explore Air, the and the Cricut Maker all have double connectors and take into consideration one-advance cutting and composing or scoring.

The Cricut Explore One is the main machine without a double connector – it has a single connector. The Cricut Explore One doesn't accompany the embellishment connector, so on the off chance that you need to utilize that you should buy it independently. At the point when you're using the Cricut Explore One for cutting and composing or scoring when it's done slicing and proceeds onward to either composing or scoring, it will stop and brief you to change out the edge lodging for the embellishment lodging.

Quick Mode

Quick Mode is another component and is just accessible with the Cricut Explore Air 2 and the Cricut Maker. It takes into consideration up to 2x faster cutting and composing when you are utilizing sure materials. Quick Mode just works with cardstock, vinyl, and iron-on vinyl, yet it permits you to complete your tasks in practically a fraction of when you are utilizing those materials. At the point when you are using different materials, the cutting time is equivalent to the next Cricut Explore models.

Versatile Tool System

With the expansion of the most up to date Cricut machine, the Cricut Maker, another lodging was presented for machine embellishments. It's known as the Adaptive Tool System! This framework can lift and turn the sharp edge during the cutting procedure. It does this dependent on the sort of material you are cutting and the kind of advantage you are utilizing. This framework is just accessible with the Cricut Maker machine.

That implies that the Adaptive Tool System can control the specific weight and speed expected to precisely cut even the trickiest materials. From flimsy tissue paper to thick textures like fleece and cowhide – the Cricut Maker can deal with them all!

This is not the same as the Cricut Explore machines, where the sharp edge hauls along the material as the tangle travels through the machine. The Cricut Maker sharp edges proceed onward their own utilizing an apparatus framework rather than simply being pulled through materials. There are two new sharp edges that lone work with the Cricut Maker – the Rotary Blade and the Knife Blade. Cricut is anticipating extending the apparatuses that work with the Adaptive Tool System. Along these lines, as new devices turn out, you won't have to refresh your machine. Instead, your machine capacities will develop as you include more apparatuses that all work with the Adaptive Tool System.

The freshest apparatuses for the framework of the versatile device are the Scoring Wheel and the Double Scoring Wheel.

Hues

Note: I continue attempting to refresh this post to include more hues as they become accessible. Be that as it may, they continue containing such a significant number of shades in all the various stores. It's challenging to keep up. In any case, I'm giving a valiant effort to keep the rundown beneath refreshed. Thanks for your comprehension.

This isn't generally a functional component of the machine, however once in a while, the shade of the device is something individuals have substantial feelings on. Each device has another scope of hues that it comes in. There are standard hues for each machine model, and afterwards, they are additionally exchange and uncommon elite hues that have been discharged. The select hues must be found at specific retailers. Here are on the whole the various hues that you can discover for each machine model:

Cricut Explore Original – It's hard to discover this machine available to be purchased any longer yet you might have the option to get it on eBay or another resale site

Green

Wild Orchid – selective to HSN (restricted version)

Cricut Explore Air

Blue

Blue-green

Gold

Wild Orchid

Cricut Explore One

Dark

Coral

Naval force Bloom

Pink Poppy

Cricut Explore Air 2

Mint

Rose – selective to JOANN

Blue – selective to Michaels

Pearl — selective to Michaels (Martha Stewart version)

Ivory and Gold – selective to HSN

Sky

Matte Black

Raspberry

Flamingo Pearl

Peacock – selective to Michaels

Sunflower – selective to Michaels

Boysenberry – selective to Michaels

Periwinkle – selective to Michaels

Coral – selective to Michaels

Cobalt – selective to JOANN

Wisteria – selective to JOANN

Cricut Maker

Dim Gray and Champagne

Blue

Rose

Cost

There is a slight evaluating contrast between the entirety of the machines as a result of their various highlights. The highest point of the line machines is the Cricut Maker and the Cricut Explore Air 2. These machines offer the most element and abilities. Since the Cricut Maker is a new one,is estimated the most elevated.

The Cricut Explore Original model is never again sold by Cricut. You can discover it on Amazon once in a while and some different spots, yet for the most part, it will be around a similar cost as a Cricut Explore Air. It's better the get the Cricut Explore Air and have the Bluetooth remote incorporated with the machine.

The financial limit inviting alternative out of the considerable number of machines is the Cricut Explore One. It will regularly go around $40-$50 not exactly different machines since it just has a single connector. This is an extraordinary alternative in the event that you need a Cricut yet don't really have the spending limit for the highest point of the line model. Or then again, on the off chance that you are an easygoing crafter and don't see yourself utilizing the Cricut a ton, and possibly simply need to have it as an apparatus for extraordinary making events. The Cricut Explore One is an extraordinary choice for a lower estimated model.

On the off chance that you believe that you would be removing bunches of subtleties plans or things like various sheets of stickers, you might need to consider getting the Cricut Explore Air 2 since it can cut in quick Mode.

Since I have been utilizing my Cricut Explore Original, I've never truly been troubled by to what extent it takes the machine to remove my venture. More often than not, it's done in a concise measure of time. I am not typically cutting experiments with multifaceted subtleties or vast amounts of minor cuts, so I don't see the speed being an issue.

The leading venture that I can think about that I make that would profit by a quicker cutting time is making printable stickers. I attempt to pack; however, many stickers onto one sheet as could be expected under the circumstances, so there are bunches of cuts and shapes for the Cricut Explore to follow.

Cutting a full page of stickers can take a great deal of time, and in the event that I would have been cutting sheet after layer continually, I would consider putting resources into the Cricut Explore Air 2. The Fast Mode takes into account 2x quicker cutting when you have the quick dial set to cardstock, vinyl, or iron-on vinyl. It would accelerate the time it takes to remove a full sheet of stickers.

You can utilize the Cricut Explore to make and cut out your own stickers! Snap for the full instructional exercise.

In the event that you need to utilize your Cricut to slice texture or to assist you with your sewing ventures, as a rule, you are going to need to put resources into the Cricut Maker. The Cricut Maker is vastly improved for cutting texture than the Cricut Explore machines.

With the Cricut Explore machines, on the off chance that you needed to slice textures, you expected to join a fusible web to the rear of the surfaces to give soundness. Presently with the Cricut Maker, the rotational cutting edge will coast over the surface and cut it without packing or tearing! No sponsorship required. The Cricut Maker can remove the entirety of your texture and sewing structures. Furthermore, there are additionally massive amounts of sewing designs in Cricut Design

Space to browse so you can make pretty much any texture venture.

Which Machine Would I Buy?

In the event that I was going to purchase a machine today, I would pick either the Cricut Explore Air or the Cricut Maker.

The Cricut Explore Air is as yet a mind-blowing machine, despite the fact that there are more up to date machines available. It is an incredible machine for somebody merely beginning with the Cricut and would make an extraordinary blessing! What's more, on the grounds that there are currently two more up to date machines, the cost for this machine has gotten substantially more reasonable. The Cricut Explore Air has all the fancy odds and ends to be a definitive making and DIY apparatus.

Since I'm a gigantic Cricut fan, the Cricut Maker is unquestionably on my list of things to get. The Cricut Maker is an incredible machine and is the leader of all the Cricut items. It can cut pretty much any material from minor fragile papers to cowhide and even wood! What's more, presently with the Adaptive Tool System, the opportunities for materials are unending. Cricut will keep on including new instruments that will all work with the Cricut Maker machine. It's a DIYer's fantasy apparatus!

I couldn't imagine anything better than to redesign my Cricut Explore Original to the Cricut Maker. Since I utilize my Cricut for vast amounts of tasks, I realize I will adore the new machine!

While the Cricut Maker is unquestionably noteworthy, it is the most costly of any machines Cricut has ever discharged. What's more, I would prefer not to guide you to go out and purchase the most expensive thing since it's expensive. I need you to buy the machine that is directly for you and your needs.

I believe that the cost for the Cricut Maker is just justified, despite all the trouble on the off chance that you are anticipating utilizing all the capacities of this mind-boggling machine. In the event that you are now a Cricut Explore client and you are hoping to move up to the following best thing — this machine is for you! Or then again on the off chance that you are new to Cricut however, you realize you'll be utilizing this machine ALL the ideal opportunity for DIY ventures, sewing activities, and tons more, than this is undoubtedly the machine for you! Or on the other hand, in the event that you love to sew and need a device that will assist you with cutting examples and plans, the Cricut Maker is your most logical option – undoubtedly. It's much improved with regards to cutting texture than the Cricut Explore machines.

In any case, on the off chance that you simply need a Cricut in light of the fact that you are searching for a fantastic cutting machine, I would stay with the Cricut Explore Air. On the off chance that you are just anticipating removing essential materials like paper, vinyl, iron-on, and other regular task materials, you will be thoroughly fine with the Cricut Explore Air. Or then again, if you realize that you'll never utilize your Cricut for cutting textures, the Cricut Explore Air is ideal for you!

The Cricut Maker would be needless excess for you, and you'd wind up spending a considerable amount of cash on a machine that you aren't utilizing to its full capacities. Fundamentally, you'd be paying for a Cricut Maker yet using it like a Cricut Explore Air. So why not merely set aside cash and purchase the Cricut Explore Air?

Whichever model you choose to go with, they are generally going to dazzle you! I realize that I was continuing forever about how astounding the new Cricut Maker is, yet that doesn't mean different machines are old junky things. They are as yet mind-blowing and excellent cutting machines. The entirety of the Cricut machines truly is the best cutting machines available, as I would see it.

I trust that this encourages you to pick the best machine for your innovative needs. Tell me in the remarks which Cricut machine you have – or which one is on your list of things to get.

# Chapter 11:
# How to use a Cricut cutter and choose the right cartridge to purchase (depending on needs and budget)

Cricut cartridges are sets of pictures and textual styles that are connected by a subject, similar to Halloween, the seashore, or springtime. Each picture set can contain many pictures, textual styles, or activities, and expenses somewhere in the range of five and thirty bucks.

With the early Cricut machines, the cartridges were plastic: physical capacity gadgets that you needed to plug into your slicing machine to utilize. Presently you can connect these cartridges, or picture sets, with your Cricut ID, and access them online through Cricut Design Space (Explore arrangement) or Cricut Craft Room (Expression arrangement). You can even buy computerized cartridges, accessing sets of pictures on the web, without stressing over managing any plastic cartridges.

Do I have to utilize cartridges for a Cricut Explore Air?

Actually no, not any longer! Acclaim Cricut, for cartridges, are never again required for the different Cricut Explore models or the Cricut Maker.

The first Cricut shaper and the Cricut Expression arrangement were intended to be utilized with physical information cartridges as independent machines—ones that don't require a P.C. or a web association. The Expression machines can be utilized with the free P.C. plan programming Cricut Craft Room. However, you are as yet constrained to pictures bought through Cricut cartridges.

The entirety of the shaper models at present sold by Cricut doesn't require cartridges. In this way, in the event that you have a Cricut Explore or the Cricut Maker, and would prefer not to need to consider a cartridge until the end of time, you are allowed to proceed onward.

Would i be able to at present utilize my cartridges with new Cricut machines?

A lady focuses on the cartridge space on a Cricut Explore.

Indeed! You can utilize all your old cartridges with any of the electronic Cricut machines. The heritage machines (never again sold by Cricut, for example, the Expression arrangement, can utilize the cartridges as they generally have, by genuinely embeddings them into the machine and utilizing the console overlay, or interfacing them to Cricut Craft Room to alter on a P.C.

The fresher machines, the Cricut Explore arrangement and the Cricut Maker can totally still utilize any cartridges you have bought from Cricut. Notwithstanding, first you need to interface them to your Cricut account, so you can get to them online through Cricut Design Space.

Peruse on to discover how!

The most effective method to Use Cartridges with the Cricut Explore Air 2

So as to utilize cartridges with the Cricut Explore Air 2, they should be connected to your Cricut account so you can get to them online with Design Space.

Cautioning: You can just connect a Cricut cartridge to a solitary Cricut account. Connecting a cartridge is

IRREVERSIBLE: you can't fix it, and you can't move it to another record. Continuously ensure you are marked into the privilege Cricut account before connecting your cartridges!

Head on over to Cricut.com/structure and sign in to Cricut Design Space on a Windows or Mac PC. You can't interface cartridges through the telephone or tablet applications.

Ensure your Cricut Explore is turned on and associated with your P.C.

Snap the menu button in the upper left (it would appear that a burger: three even bars) and select "Connection Cartridges", mostly down the menu. In Cricut Design Space, the choice for "Connection Cartridges" is featured.

Select your Cricut gadget starting from the drop menu.

When provoked, embed your cartridge into space on the left half of the Explore shaper, over the "Open" button.

A Cricut cartridge is embedded into the opening on a Cricut Explore.

After Design Space has identified the cartridge, the green "Connection Cartridge" catch will illuminate. Snap the latch to interface your cartridge.

At the point when the cartridge is connected to your Cricut account, Design Space will affirm "Cartridge connected." You would now be able to continue connecting the remainder of your cartridges, see your cartridges, or hit the X in the upper option to close the cartridge connecting exchange and come back to Cricut Design Space.

How would I discover my cartridges in Cricut Design Space?

It's anything but difficult to get to your connected cartridges and bought pictures in Cricut Design Space.

In an open canvas in Design Space, click the "Pictures" button on the menu bar to one side to open up the Images window.

Over the top, you'll see three interactive words: Images Categories Cartridges. Snap "Cartridges" to see a rundown of all the Cricut cartridges available. In Cricut Design Space, "Cartridges" is chosen in the upper right corner.

On the off chance that you need to see only the cartridges that you effectively claim, click the "Channel" button on the upper right of the Images window and select "My Cartridges." This will incorporate all free and bought cartridges. In Cricut Design Space, the separating alternative for the cartridges is chosen.

Make a point to look at the Images tab too in the event that you have bought or transferred singular pictures.

What's the distinction between physical and computerized cartridges?

Physical cartridges contain themed sets of pictures in a plastic cartridge that you genuinely embed into your cutting machine. With the Cricut Expression, you can utilize physical cartridges straightforwardly by embeddings them into the machine and utilizing the console to choose and control the pictures. You can likewise connect these physical cartridges to your Cricut account utilizing Design Space or Craft Room. When connected, you can promptly get to computerized renditions of the cartridges in the internet altering programming.

In any case, you should even now keep the physical cartridge, or if nothing else snap a couple photographs of the front and back. In the event that you ever experience difficulty getting to your connected cartridges and need to resync them, Cricut backing may request these photographs as evidence that you possess the cartridges.

Advanced cartridges are themed sets of pictures purchased on the web, and are promptly accessible through Cricut Design Space. They have no physical part, so nothing will be delivered to you, and nothing should be connected to your Cricut shaper. You can utilize these with all the ongoing Cricut machines when you are associated with the web and signed into Cricut Design Space.

Aces

Cartridges are a fantasy for a tenderfoot crafter. Making your own structures without any preparation can be astonishing, yet now and again it's somewhat scary taking a gander at a clear canvas and pondering where to begin. With cartridges, you can discover motivation effectively within reach, assembled by any occasion or subject you can think up. Cartridges are a fast and simple approach to plunge into making custom made vinyl decals and welcome cards, without spending ages fixating on the structure.

There are huge amounts of bit by bit instructional exercises you can discover to make ventures with cartridges. These are extraordinary to utilize when you are first figuring out how to utilize a Cricut. There are such huge numbers of various things to realize when you are beginning, instructional exercises make it simple by taking out all the mystery! Look at this too charming fox head produced using the 3D Animal Heads cartridge:

A 3D fox head made out of dark-coloured and green cardstock that is stating, "How you doin'?"

You can locate the full instructional exercise for making this 3D fox head at Cricut.com.

The pictures in every cartridge are deliberately chosen and well-curated. Numerous capable craftsmen have poured huge amounts of time and exertion into the making of cartridges only for you to utilize! You can believe that the pictures and text styles will be high-calibre, and work consistently with your Cricut.

There are right around 500 hundred cartridges in the Cricut Cartridge Library! Every cartridge contains various pictures and ventures that can be altered and joined with various imaginative highlights, giving a phenomenal scope of structures. There are simply such huge numbers of shapes, examples, and text styles to browse, you can generally discover something that looks extraordinary for whatever venture you are making.

Cartridges really are an incredible worth. From only a solitary cartridge, you can produce several unique structures from the base pictures. On the off chance that you feel that your Cricut cartridge assortment has been getting excessively expensive, invest more energy trying different things with the cartridges you as of now have, and utilize that imaginative worth.

Having a physical assortment of Cricut cartridges can be brilliant for discovering motivation for your next task. Rather than gazing at pictures on a screen to discover something to make, you can remain off the P.C. and peruse through a physical library of your cartridge assortment.

Cons

Before the Cricut Explore arrangement, the principal impediment of the cartridge framework was that you were constrained to what went ahead of the cartridges. Since cartridges are presently totally discretionary with the more up to date Cricut machines, this is never again an inconvenience! You can generally transfer your own structures or utilize free SVGs you find on the web.

An adorable papercraft creature head, made out of pastel cardstock.

One significant issue is that you can just connection cartridges to a solitary Cricut account. On the off chance that you are skilled cartridges, or get some from e-inlet or a second-hand store, they may as of now be connected to another person's record! Connecting cartridges is irreversible, and you can't switch what record they're connected to. So ensure you don't get fooled into purchasing cartridges you can't really use with your machine.

In the wake of purchasing a lot of cartridges, you may feel like you are secured in the Cricut brand, or perhaps with a specific machine. This is extraordinary for Cricut, however not very good for imparting to the making and

D.I.Y. people group. On the off chance that you plan with cartridges, you can only with significant effort to share your structures with others one of my preferred pieces of making new ventures! On the off chance that you utilize plain ol' SVG documents rather, they can be effectively imparted to other people and brought into the planned programming for different brands of the shaper, similar to Silhouette Studio.

The cartridges don't work the equivalent for each Cricut machine. The Expressions can utilize cartridges without the web. For the Cricut Explore Air 2, you need to connect the cartridge to your record. Furthermore, the Cricut Maker doesn't have a cartridge space! On the off chance that you need to utilize pictures from all your old cartridges with a Maker, you'll need to buy the extraordinary Cartridge Adapter from Cricut so as to connect them. (Or then again perhaps you can utilize a companion's Cricut Explore to carry out the responsibility!)

The console overlay for the Create a Critter Cricut cartridge.

F.A.Q.

Can you unlink a Cricut cartridge?

Not a chance! When a cartridge is connected to a Cricut account, it's connected until the end of time. You can't unlink or move a cartridge to another record.

Consider the possibility that my cartridge was at that point connected to Cricut Craft Room.

On the off chance that you have just connected cartridges to Cricut Craft Room to use with a Cricut Expression, they are as yet accessible for you to use with any more current machine! They are really connected to your Cricut.com account, and ought to be naturally accessible in Cricket Design Space, at www.Cricut.com/structure.

Would i be able to interface cartridges utilizing the iPhone or iPad application? Shouldn't something be said about the Android application?

No, you can just connection cartridges through Cricut Design Space on a Windows or Mac PC.

Imagine a scenario in which I've just connected my cartridges to my Gypsy. How would I move cartridges from my Gypsy to my Cricut account?

You can move cartridges from your Gypsy to your Cricut account by connecting your Gypsy to Craft Room and synchronizing the gadget. Every one of your cartridges will be transferred to your Cricut account, and be available through either Craft Room or Design Space. Ensure your Gypsy is enlisted to a similar email account you use for Cricut.com.

Where are my text styles?

Heaps of Cricut clients have whined that they can't discover textual styles they bought on the web or textual styles that originated from the physical textual style cartridges they connected to their Cricut account.

Have no dread, your text styles are here! So as to see the textual styles you can utilize, you first need to have some content set.

In Cricut Design Space, place a book box by tapping the "Content" button on the menu bar to one side, and composing in your content.

Presently when you have your content chosen, you should see "Textual style" at the upper left, alongside a drop-down menu that will permit you to choose any text style.

At the point when you select "Text style" at the upper left, you will see a mammoth rundown of all the free textual styles, all your bought text styles, and all the textual styles you can give it a shot and purchase. To discover just the text styles you as of now have, click "Channel" in the upper right of the Font window, and select "My Fonts."

# Chapter 12:
# How to make modifications to your design by editing the images and fonts

Prepare in light of the fact that toward the finish of this article, you will ace how to alter the message in Cricut Design Space like PRO! I need to show you how to angle and engage you with the information to think of cool thoughts all alone!

Content it's an immense arrangement in any plan, you can achieve such a great amount with it, and that is the reason you have to get hands-on and get familiar with all the conceivable outcomes you have with the Cricut Machine.

On this post, you will gain proficiency with the thinking and kind of rationale of how content functions in Cricut Design Space, at that point we will apply those ideas in a stage to step instructional exercise.

Gracious!...

Gracious! What's more, to make sure you know, I likewise have a FREE developing library with huge amounts of printables and SVG documents fit to be cut.

I would cherish for you to have the option to gain admittance to every one of them. It's 100% Free for my daydreamers (otherwise known as supporters) look at a live review here, or get access here.

How about we begin!

Page Content show

Content Basics

Something that I like the most about content is that you can customize all that you need and your heart wants.

Learning the nuts and bolts and further developed alternatives you have inside the Cricut Design Space territory will permit you to customize things, yet in addition, doing it wonderfully!

Including and Editing Text

First of all!

With the goal for you to add content to the structure zone, you have to tap on the T (content) symbol situated on the left board of the canvas.

In the wake of clicking a little box will show up, and this is the place you would type your content.

Screen capture for how to include the message in Cricut Design Space

To add content, click on the content catch situated on the left board.

On the off chance that you as of now have composed some content, you can without much of a stretch alter it by double-tapping the content itself in the canvas territory.

Screen capture to alter previously made content.

Double-tap on content to alter the substance

Altering Menu Overview

There are endless ways for you to alter content, however, for this instructional exercise we are going to centre with the choices given in the altering menu; particularly the symbols that are set apart in pink.

Try not to be modest. After you are finished with this instructional exercise feel free to attempt different alternatives, I guarantee your PC won't break. 😜

Screen capture of altering content menu in Design Space

Altering Menu – Focus on Pink Areas

These are the themes we will cover in subtleties.

Linetype and Fill

Text style

Text Style and Font size

Letter Space and Line Space

Arrangement

Bend

Progressed

Linetype and Fill for Text

Linetype and fill will fundamentally advise your machine how to cut or treat your materials when you press Make it.

Fundamentally you will have 5 alternatives joined (3 Linetype and 2 with a fill)

Linetype

On this drop-down menu, you will have three choices:

Screen capture of linetype drop-down menu Cricut Design Space

Cut: Will advise your machine to cut. Here you can change hues as well, and each shading will speak to an alternate material shading.

Draw: With this choice, you are advising your Cricut to draw, and for this, you will require the Cricut Pens. So when you press make it; your content will be drawn and not cut.

Score: When choosing this choice, your content will be scored, and for this sort of impact you need either the scoring stylus or potentially the scoring wheel. This final one is for the Cricut Maker as it were!

Fill

Screen capture of Fill alternative in Cricut Design Space

This alternative could be somewhat more befuddling. Be that as it may, here I am to make it simple for you!

Fill is just for the PRINT at that point CUT alternative, and it's possibly initiated when you have Cut as a linetype.

No Fill: implies that you won't print anything, so on the off chance that printing something out isn't you aim, at that point overlook this setting.

Print: this implies you will printing your plan and afterwards cutting it when you click here, you would now be able to pick your print type by tapping on the little shading square.

Shading: pick shading to print in any shading you need your content to be.

Example: select example on the off chance that you need your content to be loaded up with your own or Cricut designs.

Screen capture of Linetype and fill choices for content in Cricut configuration space.

Content Options with Linetype and Fill

Textual style Types

Each time you type something, Cricut Sans will be the default textual style. On the off chance that you need to change the text style, simply click on the Fonts drop-down menu and pick your preferred textual style.

Screen capture of picking various kinds of text styles in Cricut Design Space

Check various approaches to channel text styles!

Remember that not all textual styles are free on the off chance that you have Cricut Access you can utilize the greater part of them. Notwithstanding, some of them should be bought before cutting your undertaking.

In the event that you don't have the foggiest idea what Cricut Access is, make a point to peruse this extraordinary guide I set up.

In the event that you need to adhere to free textual styles make a point to channel by "My Fonts" (This will incorporate your framework textual styles and some Cricut Fonts that Cricut may have free right now.

Something truly cool about Cricut Fonts is the composition and Multi-layer Fonts.

Composing text styles are incredible for Cricut Pens, since they will give a hand attracted impact to your undertaking, and multi-layer textual styles are a sort textual style that comprises of at least 2 layers.

I will clarify what is multi-layer text style in the propelled choices symbol.

The Major Difference between Cricut Fonts and System Fonts

There's a major distinction between the Cricut and System text styles, and that is the Cricut Fonts are intended to fit the entirety of the capability of your machine.

You have the Writing – as a text style – and the Multi-Layer choices.

Sure you can compose with your framework text styles – by changing the Linetype for a draw – however it would look progressively like a blueprint of the textual style as opposed to a manually written impact.

Screen capture demonstrating the distinction between Cricut Fonts and System Fonts in Cricut Design Space

Cricut Fonts versus System Fonts

Text Style

Screen capture of Font Style in Cricut Design Space

At the point when you click on text style, you will be given a drop-down menu. Most normal alternatives are: Regular, Bold, Italic and Bold Italic.

In any case, in the event that you are utilizing Cricut Fonts, you may have less or more alternatives like Writing.

Text dimension and Letter Spacing

Top Panel Font Spacing and size Cricut Design Space

As the name says it, the text dimension will permit you to change the size of your chose content.

Letter Space is truly cool since you can change the space between letters.

Line Space is amazingly cool also, yet this time you can either increment or reduction the length of content lines.

Screen capture of how letter space and Lines Space work in Cricut Design Space

Unique Design in Blue – Letter Space in Yellow – Line Space in Pink

Letter Spacing to Fix Script

Something that letter separating is great at is to fix your cursive text styles.

The first occasion when I attempted to make a venture with a written by hand text style, I didn't comprehend why it looked so strange and terrible. Right up 'til the present time I despite everything don't comprehend...

The thing is that of course all cursive text styles will be scattered. In any case, not stresses, take a gander at the screen capture down howl to figure out how to fix this issue.

Screen capture of how to fix cursive text style dispersing in Cricut Design Space

Fix Cursive Letter Spacing

Compose your ideal content and select your cursive text style. Recollect, of course, all letters will be scattered.

Select the content and diminish the letter dispersing, to get it practically great. There will be a few letters covering one another. However, we will fix this in a minute.

Select your content and this time click on cutting edge and select ungroup to letters. Presently you will have the option to move each letter all alone. For this, I moved the letter C.

In the event that you were going to cut your venture at the present time, all letters would be removed separately. To make this a solitary word, select the entirety of the letters and snap on the weld alternative situated at the base of the right – layers – board of the canvas region.

Note: You will study the propelled alternatives shortly!

Content Alignment

This choice gives you three unique other options:

Left: Selected content will be adjusted to one side

Focus: Selected content will be focused

Right: Selected content will be adjusted to one side

Screen Shot for content arrangement in Cricut Design Space

Adjust Left Yellow – Align Right Pink – Align Center Blue

Bend Text

I love this component! Bending content can add an additional touch to any structure. Be that as it may, this alternative is just accessible for one line of content at that point; no passages!

Select your content line and play with the bend alternative. The further you are from the middle, the more bent appearance you will add to your content.

Screen capture of how to bend a line of content in Cricut Design Space

Propelled Options

This is by a long shot one of my preferred choices, and you may believe is troublesome in light of the name of this symbol!

For this model, I am utilizing a Multi-Layer text style called A Frightful Affair. This text style is made out of two layers. An external – dark – and inward – yellow – one. Each layer speaks to an alternate material.

Utilizing this text style, how about we perceive how every one of the propelled choices works.

Screen capture of Advanced Options in Cricut Design Space

This is a Multi-Layer Font

Ungroup to layers: this choice is just accessible on multi-layers textual styles. At the point when you click on this alternative, you can isolate the entirety of the layers that make up the text style and alter them independently.

This is extraordinary on the off chance that you just need to utilize a specific layer of content.

Ungroup to lines: If you have to compose a passage yet need all content lines on their own, this instrument will be your closest companion.

Compose your passage, adjust and space your textual styles and afterwards click on ungroup to lines; Then you can alter each line of content all alone!

Ungroup to Letters: this choice permits you to isolate each letter into an alternate layer; it very well may be applied to a section, line of content, or simply any word.

Screen capture of how to ungroup to layers, lines and letters works in Cricut Design Space.

Ungroup to Layers, Lines and Letters Graphic

Note that when you separate to lines and letters, the text style kept the multi-layer characteristic. In this way, If you have a multi-layer text style, you can ungroup to layers in the wake of utilizing either ungroup to lines or letters.

Presently, Let's Put in Practice what we realized!

It's the ideal opportunity for you to place practically speaking what you simply realized!

All the way we are going to use the same number of apparatuses as we can to accomplish the plan on the screen capture directly down underneath.

Try not to be hesitant to switch things up. The most ideal approach to learn is by attempting new things constantly.

Screen capture of definite bit by bit instructional exercise in Cricut Design Space

We should get moving!

Stage 1 – Add Text

First, we are going to include the accompanying section.

LEARNING AND PRACTICING NEW

THINGS ARE DEFINITELY SOME OF

MY FAVORITE THINGS IN THE WORLD

Here we are attempting to keep the entirety of the lines of the section a similar length. It's not absolutely conceivable, but rather we will fix this later.

Instructional exercise Screenshot of stage 1 - include a message in Cricut Design Space.

Stage 1 – Add Text

Stage 2 – Choose your text style

How about we select a cuter text style!

Snap-on text style, at that point, investigate your choices by separating each choice. I went with Avenida Com.

Screen capture of - Step 2 - Choose your text style - Cricut Design Space

Stage 2 – Choose your text style

Stage 3 – Ungroup to lines

Recollect when I said we were unable to bend content with a passage?

Since you can just bend content with lines of words, we will choose our section, and afterwards, we are going to tap on Advanced and pick ungroup to lines.

Now you will have the option to alter each and every line all alone!

Instructional exercise Screenshot of - Step 3 Ungroup to lines - in Cricut Design Space

Stage 3 – Ungroup to lines

Be that as it may, as should be obvious right now they are not a similar length, and we need them to be on the grounds that in any case, our structure wouldn't look even.

Stage 4 – Use Letter Spacing

We have to make the entirety of the lines a similar length. I like to have the longest queue direct the size of different lines.

To do this, select the mainline and change the letter space until the line looks a similar size to the centre one. When you are done, rehash a similar procedure with the third line.

Instructional exercise Screenshot of - Step 4 - Use Letter Spacing - in Cricut Design Space

Stage 4 – Use Letter Spacing

Stage 5 – Let's bend some content.

Here we are going to include our breathtaking impact!

Select the principal line of content and snap-on bend, and type - 5.104, this will make the line to bend down.

At that point, we will choose the second line of content; however, this time, we are going to type 5.104. This will make the line bend up.

At long last, for the third line of the content, we are going to rehash something very similar we did with the mainline. Snap-on bend and type - 5.104

Instructional exercise Screenshot of - Step 5 bending content in Cricut Design Space

Stage 5 – Let's bend some content.

Stage 6 – Organize the entirety of the components

Presently sort out the entirety of the component like the screen capture down beneath.

Instructional exercise Screenshot of Step 6 - Organize the entirety of the components in Cricut Design Space

Stage 6 – Organize the entirety of the components

Stage 7 – Let's play with Linetype and Fill.

Normally you would adhere to one Linetype, however with the end goal of this instructional exercise, we are going to utilize the draw, and cut and print choices.

For the primary line, I chose to draw as a linetype and afterwards for shading I went with a light turquoise.

Instructional exercise Screenshot of Step 7 - Let's play with Linetype and Fill/Draw Linetype/in Cricut Design Space.

Stage 7 – Let's play with Linetype and Fill/Draw Linetype

For the subsequent line, I went with Cut as linetype to actuate the fill alternative. At that point, I chose print as fill and a turquoise shading.

Instructional exercise Screenshot of Step 7 - Let's play with Linetype and Fill/Linetype: Cut - Fill: Print, Print type: shading/in Cricut Design Space

Stage 7 – Let's play with Linetype and Fill/Linetype: Cut – Fill: Print, Print type: shading

For the last line, I needed to investigate designs! So I chose slice as linetype to actuate the fill alternative, and afterwards, I changed the print type for design.

There are numerous alternatives you can choose from; however, I needed to stay with a turquoise design.

Instructional exercise Screenshot of Step 7 - Let's play with Linetype and Fill/Linetype: Cut - Fill: Print, print type: Pattern/in Cricut Design Space

Stage 7 – Let's play with Linetype and Fill/Linetype: Cut – Fill: Print, print type: Pattern

That is it! You are a Pro Now!

So...

What did you all think?

Do you feel increasingly certain with altering content at this point?

What sort of ventures would you say you are going to make since you are a Pro at altering content in Cricut Design Space?

# Conclusion

All good things with a beginning, they say, must have an end. Well, it has been a pleasurable journey writing this book. I know you have learnt a lot. Kindly write me if you feel there were some things you would rather I talked about. I would love to hear from you.

Printed in the USA
CPSIA information can be obtained
at www.ICGtesting.com
LVHW012146240924
792064LV00029B/912